OT דמיונות

nd the Cultural Imagination

tha Baskind, General Editor

al Board
Baskin, University of Oregon
Biale, University of California, Davis
Kogman-Appel, Ben-Gurion University of the Negev
Levitt, Temple University
avans, Amherst College
Stern, Harvard University

s in the Dimyonot series explore the intersections, and interstices, of Jewish
nce and culture. These projects emerge from many disciplines—including
tory, language, literature, music, religion, philosophy, and cultural studies—
erse chronological and geographical locations. Each volume, however,
gates the multiple and evolving representations of Judaism and Jewishness,
Jews and non-Jews, over time and place.

The Objects That Remain

The Objects That Remain

Laura Levitt

The Pennsylvania State University Press
University Park, Pennsylvania

Sections of this book were previously published as "Revisiting the Property Room: A Humanist Perspective on Doing Justice and Telling Stories," *Conversations: An Online Journal of the Center for the Study of Material and Visual Cultures of Religion* (2015); "Miki Kratsman, Diptych from *The Resolution of the Suspect*," *MAVCOR Journal* 2, no. 1 (2018); "Evidence: Doing Justice," *Bulletin for the Study of Religion* 41 (November 2012): 37–44; and "Ritual and Rites in Holocaust Commemoration: A Silence in the Archive," *Bulletin for the Study of Religion*, February 12, 2016.

The views or opinions expressed in this book, and the context in which the images are used, do not necessarily reflect the views or policy of, nor imply approval or endorsement by, the United States Holocaust Memorial Museum.

Library of Congress Cataloging-in-Publication Data

Names: Levitt, Laura, 1960– author.
Title: The objects that remain / Laura Levitt.
Other titles: Dimyonot (University Park, Pa.)
Description: University Park, Pennsylvania : The Pennsylvania State University Press, [2020] | Series: Dimyonot: Jews and the cultural imagination | Includes bibliographical references and index.
Summary: "A personal memoir and examination of the ways in which the material remains of violent crimes, from rape to genocide, inform our experience of, and thinking about, trauma and loss"—Provided by publisher.
Identifiers: LCCN 2020029004 | ISBN 9780271087825 (cloth)
Subjects: LCSH: Levitt, Laura, 1960– | Violent crimes—Psychological aspects. | Personal belongings—Psychological aspects. | Psychic trauma. | Loss (Psychology)
Classification: LCC HV6493.L48 2020 | DDC 362.8801/9—dc23
LC record available at https://lccn.loc.gov/2020029004

The Pennsylvania State University Press is a member of the Association of University Presses.

It is the policy of The Pennsylvania State University Press to use acid-free paper. Publications on uncoated stock satisfy the minimum requirements of American National Standard for Information Sciences—Permanence of Paper for Printed Library Material, ansi z39.48–1992.

In honor of my mother,

Phyllis Levitt, and all those

who hold her memory and

carry her legacy forward.

A sudden death is one way—a terrible way, I suppose—of freezing the details of a life. While writing *Jane* I became amazed by the way one act of violence had transformed an array of everyday items—a raincoat, a pair of pantyhose, a paperback book, a wool jumper—into numbered pieces of evidence, into talismans that threatened at every turn to take on allegorical proportions.

—**Maggie Nelson**, *The Red Parts*, **120**

Contents

Acknowledgments

First and foremost, I thank my friends who brought me to this project and to Maggie Nelson, Christina Crosby, and Janet Jakobsen. I thank Maggie Nelson for her inspiring work. I am also indebted to the many artists and scholars whose works continue to deepen and sharpen my thinking, most especially Edmund de Waal, Svetlana Boym, Larry Sultan, and Mike Mandel, Kelly Sultan, Robert Jan van Pelt, and Miriam Greenbaum, Aliza Svartz, Jonathan Safran Foer, Dubravka Ugrešić, Daniel Burns, James Young, Oren Stier, Jennifer Scheper Hughes, Kathleen Biddick, Ariella Azoulay, Miki Kratsman, Leora Auslander, Liliane Weissberg, Jennifer Hansen-Glucklich, Oren Stier, Maurizia Boscagli, Deborah Lipstadt, Irena Klepfisz, Tania Oldenhage, Joan Scott, Bożena Shallcross, Jeffery Shandler, Peter Stallybrass, Sally Promey, Alexander Nagel, and Israel Jacob Yuval.

For their extraordinary editorial support, I want to thank profoundly my editor at Penn State University Press, Patrick Alexander, and my series editor, Samantha Baskind, for believing in this project and working so closely with me as I completed the final iteration of this book. I am grateful to Alex Vose and the whole production team at the Press for all of their work on this book.

I am indebted to many dear friends, family members, and colleagues, but most especially to the following gifted readers, editors, and profound supporters for their critical engagement: Ruth Ost, Dawn Skorczewski, Irving Levitt (who listened to so many iterations of various pieces of this project over a very long time!), David Harrington Watt, Miriam Peskowitz, Susan E. Shapiro, and Deborah Luepnitz. I thank Cecelia Cancellaro for helping me find my voice at a critical moment. And I honor the memory of Deborah Lamb, who taught me to believe in myself early on. I carry her memory with me in all that I do.

I have special gratitude for the folks who do the work of holding, many of whom took me into their worlds and taught me so much. These folks include Jane Klinger, Krista Hegburg, and Travis Roxlau at the USHMM, Joseph Latta at the IAPE, and Elizabeth Peirce at the Philadelphia Museum of Art.

I want to thank Sally Promey and Emily Floyd at the Center for the Study of Material and Visual Cultures of Religion (MAVCOR) at Yale University and Byron Lee and Patricia Way for early editing. I am grateful to Leonard Primiano and Lisa Ratmansky for pushing me to learn about relics in the South of France, and to so many wonderful colleagues and friends who read and engaged with my work over the many years of this project: Rebecca Alpert, Lila Corwin Berman, Anne Létourneau, Zak Braiterman (it is about Justice), Cara Rock Singer, Jerry Singer, Rachael Kamel, Stephenie Young, Brett Kaplan, Jim Hicks, Monica Popescu, Alicia Partnoy, Erin McGlothlin, Gary Weissman, Bradley Prager, Danielle Christmas, Elizabeth Castelli, Martin Kavka, Ann Pellegrini, Julija Sukys, David Shneer, Marla Segal, Rachel Havrelock, Ken Koltun-Fromm, Jonathan Boyarin, Elissa Sampson, Daniel Boyarin, Pika Ghosh, Deborah Dash Moore, Tracy Fessenden, Marian Ronan, Kelly Baker, Jodi Eichler Levine, Samira Mehta, Carolyn Kitch, Avi Alpert, Molly Farneth, Aniko Szucs, Kathryn Lofton, Ora Gelley, David Levitt, Ken Salzmann, Brett Krutzsch, Robert Granat, and Enrique Cintron.

I am also grateful for the various cohorts of students who worked closely with me in Evidence: The Course, a special research seminar in the University Honors Program at Temple University. Reading Maggie Nelson with all of you was extraordinary.

This book has benefited greatly from various talks I have given over the years, including the Aronov Lecture at the University of Alabama in March 2017, the Kwartler Family Lecture at Princeton University in March 2015, and the Lillian Solotkin Lecture at Indiana University in February 2014. I also presented portions of this work in the South of France among my beloved Creoles at the Chateau d'Aragon in 2015, and with Ken Koltun-Fromm, Martin Kavka, and David Harrington Watt at a humanities conference in Prague in 2017. I presented a version of chapter 3 at the Religion in America Seminar at Columbia University in 2016. Other talks include presentations at the American Academy of Religion, the North American Association for the Study of Religion, and the Association for Jewish Studies, and at the University of Rochester, Syracuse University, the Center for the Humanities at Temple University, a comparative literature conference at Princeton University, the University of Pennsylvania, the University of North Carolina at Chapel Hill, and Lehigh University.

I benefited greatly by participating in Literary Responses to Genocide in the Post-Holocaust Era, a Summer Research Workshop at the United States Holocaust Memorial Museum's Mandel Center for Advanced Holocaust Studies, August 4–15, 2014. And I am honored to be a part of Material Economies of Religion in the Americas, a multiyear project at MAVCOR, where I have benefited from long and deep conversations with many extraordinary colleagues.

Finally, I am grateful to Temple University and the College of Liberal Arts for granting me two study leaves and a summer research grant to work on this book. The grant and first leave came early in the project, while the second enabled me to complete final edits. Many people at Temple made this work possible, too many to name, among them faculty, staff, and students in the Department of Religion, the Jewish Studies Program, the Feinstein Center for American Jewish History, the Gender, Sexuality, and Women's Studies Program, and the Temple University Honors Program.

Prelude
An Affection for Objects, a Memory of Blood

I have always liked things. I have a special fondness for shoes and cloth-ing. As a child, I even talked to my shoes. I was especially attached to my school shoes in the days when we all had a special pair to be worn every day for the entire year. We would go shoe shopping every fall and I would get to pick them out. The hardest part was coming home and having to displace the prior year's shoes. I felt sorry for them. It hurt to say goodbye.

I had strong feelings about other everyday pieces of clothing, espe-cially my childhood undershirts, a white cotton sleeveless variety with a bow on the front. Inside the back was the tag. The bow made the front special and I felt sorry for the back. Not only did it never get to be in front, but it also had no adornment. As a very young child, I taught myself a trick to help make up for this discrepancy. I learned how to put my undershirts on inside out and upside down. This allowed the back to be in front at least once each day as I put the undershirt on. I still tend to put on tops in this manner, inside out and upside down, and I have been embarrassed when caught unconsciously doing this seem-ingly abnormal thing in a public place, like the locker room at the gym. In these awkward moments, I am often abruptly reminded that this is not the way most people put on their shirts.

When I was about four going on five, my family visited my grand-mother in her Long Island home. My grandmother lived up a hill, and a very long, intricate cement staircase led up to the house, punctuated with rocks on the railings and turrets at the landings that made the whole property look like a castle. We had to walk down those stairs as we said goodbye and returned to our car. It was a long haul for my four-year-old legs and even longer for my little brother.

I was the big sister. My brother was eighteen months younger, and although I don't remember exactly what happened, as we descended the stairs that day, he fell. I may have pushed him. Or I may have wished that I had pushed him, but when it happened, I was completely unnerved, overcome with guilt for whatever ill wishes I may have harbored just moments before the fall.

He landed on his chin and had to be rushed to the hospital for stitches. That was the first of three falls he took on those steps, but this, the first, lingers in my memory. I could not forgive myself for what had happened and focused on all the blood. En route to the hospital, I said the word over and over, *blood, blood, blood, blood*. I said it so many times that I could no longer distinguish the meaning of the word from the sound of the letters as I enunciated them. I do not remember my brother covered in blood. I have no recollection of his stained clothing. I only remember repeating the word to myself over and over again. And, after he came home, I remember the big bandage on his chin. I recall that it scared the kids on our block. In the past, he'd been known as a biter, and the wound served to call attention to his mouth once again.

Introduction

The Afterlife of Objects

It was early August when I took the Metro out to a suburban station to meet the chief conservator of the United States Holocaust Memorial Museum (USHMM). She was taking me to the museum's off-site storage facility. I would spend the day in this most unlikely space. As I entered the nondescript suburban building—the museum's off-site repository had not yet moved into its new state-of-the art facility—I was struck by its bland character, a deliberate choice. This was my impression until I entered the first of many rooms and, eventually, the vast storage space that housed so much of the museum's collection. As if I had entered into a folded Le Sac bag, it was hard to believe that the building could be so large.

In that first room, a conservation space, I watched a woman seated beside an ironing board, sewing intently. She was working on a damaged blue-and-white-striped prisoner uniform. Of course, I had never been this close to one of these iconic garments. I thought about the uniforms I had seen on display and those I had seen in photographs. This jacket was much more elaborate than any I had ever seen. It was carefully tailored with many seams and pockets, but it was also in terrible shape. There were huge holes and tears in it (why is this word the same as tears?). These wounds were the focus of the seamstress's careful attention. The room was electric with the energy that crackled from this fragile object, and I was deeply affected by the experience.

Fig. 1. Artifact. Photo: United States Holocaust Memorial Museum.

In my last book, I wrote about a different kind of Holocaust object, family photographs and the allure of those precious traces of life before.[1] I wrote about holding and touching such photographs, the ways in which many people carried these images with them. I built on powerful scholarly works that described these attachments in terms of haptic cinema and photography, the touching of images, but now I find myself homing in to consider clothing and other material objects as much more intimate. These are objects that cover and hold our bodies. We wear these textiles. We live inside them. The longer we inhabit them, the more of us they contain. As Maggie Nelson suggests, millions of traces of our DNA, in skin cells, sweat, piss, blood, saliva, tears, permeate such garments.[2] But clothing that is worn day in and day out for long periods of time is also marked in a different way. It is shaped by our bodies. Not only were these uniforms worn constantly, but because they were handed out haphazardly, they often did not fit and so were carefully tailored by the very prisoners who wore them, who used whatever was at hand to try to make them fit. The uniform jacket I saw being mended was unusual in its intricate tailoring. It was altered to fit a specific person.

The camp uniforms held in the USHMM collection are so fragile that careful efforts must be made simply to keep them from disintegrating. And because the bodies of those who inhabited these garments have been missing for so long, in order to preserve them, to keep them from falling apart, each uniform has its own body-shaped hanger. These effigies are custom fit. They are specially made for each jacket, shirt, or pair of pants. These stuffed, mannequin-like hanging figures help take the stress off fragile seams and frayed panels. The prisoners are gone but the hangers convey a semblance of their presence. In reverse logic, the bodies beneath the fabric protect the garment, not the other way around.

Because these pieces of clothing are also witnesses to the atrocities performed on those who wore them, they attest to those crimes. They constitute a form of criminal as well as historical evidence. Bound to those bodies and those legacies, they offer silent testimony, but their presence in the museum is not simply material.

An aura emanates from these intimate articles of clothing. Once an abiding presence in the lives of those who wore them, these garments carry the traces of those now absent bodies. Such haptic connections are what attract us to these tainted pieces of clothing. Not unlike religious relics whose proximity to the bodies of saints and martyrs makes them holy, these garments hold and embody the horrors they witnessed and the memory of the lives lost. They transmit a semblance of what happened to the now ghostly figures whose shapes come back to us in the form of hanging effigies. These modern relics carry a kind of living presence. They hold traces of the blood, the sweat, the tears of those whose lives were brutally violated. They continue to bristle with meaning.

The sacred status of these pieces of clothing is bound up in visceral bodily connections similar to those that inhere in other sacred objects, such as the contact relic, the cloth that touched the martyr, the clothing that revered figures wore when they were tortured or killed. And although this notion of the relic is bound to a profoundly Christian legacy of reverence for objects, its allure is more pervasive.[3] In part, this book is about the lingering afterlives of Christian notions of the sanctity of such objects.

Let me elaborate on this strange connection. I recently stumbled onto a striking example of precisely this phenomenon. As I began reading Israeli photographer Miki Kratsman's *The Resolution of the Suspect* (2016), a book of haunting images about the horrors of the Israeli occupation of the Palestinian territories, I was struck by the ways in which Kratsman and his collaborator, the scholar of visual culture Ariella Azoulay, enact their engagement with this subject. Through photography, they show the compelling attraction of contemporary bloody garments in their attempt to address the violence of the occupation.

As I began looking through the pages of Kratsman's book, I was taken aback to find an image from another time and place, an image reframed by the photographer, *Francois Aubert's Shirt of Emperor Maximilian of Mexico*. This stark historical image depicts the shirt the emperor wore at his execution on June 19, 1867, in Queretaro, Mexico. What is striking is that this Christian-inflected image was so crucial to Kratsman's project.[4]

In Kratsman's text, the Aubert image is part of a diptych that pairs two photographs of tainted shirts accompanied by bright red handwritten inscriptions. Each photograph is the trace of a dead martyr. Atop the historical image, the text reads all in capital letters: "Although Aubert wasn't allowed to photograph the actual execution, he at least managed to document the 'scene of the crime' afterwards." Running down the inner margin of the page, we read in the same shaky, bright red handwriting, "In the tradition of Christian reverence for relics, Aubert placed the emperor's shirt in the center of his composition" (fig. 2).[5]

It was startling to find this overt invocation of a Christian tradition used as the connecting tissue between the two portions of this diptych. Here was an aging relic of a politically problematic figure, an emperor no less, a colonizer, alongside another image of "late photography," a portrait of the jacket of a contemporary Palestinian *shahid*, or martyr. Together, these images not only speak to the allure of bloody garments as contemporary relics; they overtly point to a Christian tradition of reverence for tainted objects as an ongoing and shared communal practice.

LATE PHOTOGRAPHY

ALTHOUT AUBERT WASN'T ALLOWED TO PHOTOGRAPH THE ACTUAL EXECUTION, HE AT LEAST MANAGED TO DOCUMENT THE 'SCENE OF THE CRIME' AFTERWARDS...

IN THE TRADITION OF CHRISTIAN REVERENCE FOR RELICS, AUBERT PLACED THE EMPERORS SHIRT IN THE CENTER OF HIS COMPOSITION.

Fig. 2. Diptych from Miki Kratsman, *The Resolution of the Suspect*, 2016. Digital print. Courtesy of Miki Kratsman.

I am struck by the persistence of this overtly Catholic understanding of the bodily, the tactile relationship between such intimate objects and persons who suffer. Even in Kratsman's work about men whose politics and practices are far from innocent, such remains nevertheless reverberate. They hold these violent legacies, allowing us to imagine the people who wore them. In these ways, the objects become holy.

Like the woman mending the camp uniform in the museum's storage facility, those who perform such rites assume a reverential attitude to their task. For these keepers of accounts, the work is a calling. Their jobs harken back to an earlier historical moment when conservation began. Once upon a time, the preservation of Christian relics, the soiled clothing of Christian saints and martyrs in late antique and medieval churches, was the work of conservators.[6]

The trace. The relic. We often approach such objects with reverence. These remains are evidence of crimes both great and small. The striped uniform, the bloody hoody, each allows us to stitch connections between ourselves and these different violent legacies. Abiding affective engagements reside in these tattered objects.

Our tongues falter to explain how an event so expansive in scope as the genocide of the Holocaust shares features with an intimate and personal assault upon a single individual. The two things do not correlate. And yet these crimes stand next to each other; they touch precisely where the material artifacts mark us and enable us to retell these narratives.

The story before you is about trauma and loss and how material objects embody such suffering. It is also a tale of life after such violence and the things, the artifacts and the places, that make them manifest. Such objects keep the event tangible, suspended, and within our reach. This resonance between artifacts and their power to witness to the crimes against humanity, against individuals, and their ability to make holy the profane, is the essence of this volume.

Atlanta, November 1989

Early in the evening on the first Tuesday in November 1989, I was raped in my home in Atlanta, Georgia. As it turned out, this happened just as the Berlin Wall was about to fall. A strange man broke into my home, hid, and then attacked me. I screamed, and this only exacerbated his rage. He choked me. And then he raped me in my own bed. He threatened to kill me.

At the time, I was a graduate student at Emory completing my doctoral studies in religion. After the police finally arrived on the scene—itself a protracted and exasperating experience—they began to ask questions and collect evidence. But I need to say that the police came late, too late to apprehend the suspect. Not only had I waited on hold with 911 until I finally got through to the police, but I later learned that my landlady, having heard my cries, had also called the police to no avail. She too could not get through to report the crime in process. This is a gap in time I still cannot fully fathom. By the time the police arrived, the man was long gone.

Before I was taken to Grady Hospital, a large urban public institution, the only hospital in the vicinity equipped to deal with rape—and, I should add, the only hospital in the region with an AIDS clinic—I remember the police in my apartment. I was taken to Grady for a rape exam only after the Atlanta police had combed the scene for evidence. They attempted to take fingerprints from my refrigerator after I told them that the rapist had opened it. They also gathered other evidence. They took the comforter and some of the sheets that had been on my bed, and after the rape exam at the hospital, I believe, they also took possession of various pieces of my clothing, including my sweatpants and underwear.

But here my memory falters. I hardly remember the order of these events or what the police took. What I do know is that once they left, I threw away the rest of the clothing I had been wearing. I placed these items in a dumpster outside the hospital. At least this is how I remember it, although none of these items appear in any police documents. None of my possessions are listed in the inventory from the crime scene, for example, on the official police report. There are other discrepancies in the case file; one is my address at the time. The crime scene is listed incorrectly on the first page of this official document. The correct address does appear later in the report, but without comment. I only received a copy of this report in the fall of 2014, after I filed a request for information with the Atlanta police about my case and my evidence. To date, nothing has been found, neither the evidence procured from my rape kit nor any of the clothing or bedding taken from my home and my person that night. These items no longer appear to be accessible. I do not know what happened to any of them. Nor do I know whether my rape kit was ever processed. That information cannot be verified. I can only assume that it was not.[7]

Nevertheless, even as I have learned that these possessions are no longer accessible, I am moved by my memory, by the imprint of these once tactile everyday objects on how I think about this past and the fact that I had for so many years forgotten all about them.

What I have learned is that these objects seem to have been lost in the confusion of various moves between storage facilities in and around Atlanta in the intervening thirty-something years since that November night.

Within days of my rape, I found myself staying in a renovated 1920s bungalow just a few blocks from my house, the home of the man I was falling in love with, a potter. It was there that I began to get used to my altered life. I had not awakened. Instead, I spent those first few days in the main room of the house, an oddly disco-like open glass enclosure. It was there that I watched the Berlin Wall come down. I saw it over and over again, reflected in all those panes of glass. Nightfall came early, so the television screen was all over those glass walls. My world had been shattered alongside this world-historic event. Nothing was the same. The whole world was off kilter. Even then, I struggled with how to navigate this new terrain.

Clothing taken. Relics, bloody garments, handmade earthenware bowls, loving gifts, and the places where they were given—a first-floor apartment, a renovated house, city streets in a once divided landscape— matter. Held in such material containers, the trauma is made concrete. These tangible objects testify to the fact that these events are not a figment of the imagination. They are one important way we know that these events actually happened, that this is not a dream.

Afterlives of Trauma, Different Dreams

In *Jane: A Murder*, a book of narrative poems, Maggie Nelson suggests that violence and trauma pierce consciousness, leaving in their wake holes that cannot be filled. And in this netherworld, the boundaries between dreaming and waking become porous. Nelson's book is bound up in the landscape between dreaming and waking life. Intermingled in the text is the poet's own life, lived under the shadow of the murder of her mother's sister, Jane Mixer, a woman Nelson never met. The narrative Nelson forms about her aunt's life and death, created in her absence, is this poetry book. The story is cobbled together from the shards and traces of what was left. Just one singular act of violence leaves a scar that crosses a generation.

In a poem titled "The Gap," Nelson explains that there are "holes in time" that are "the space made / by a lost word." In the wake of such blackness, there is no sight. One can only hear if one listens *"hard enough,"* *"the rhythm / of the ache."*[8] For me, this aching dark terrain is life after trauma and violence, and it is, perhaps, as Nelson suggested, experienced most vividly through dreams.

Although I am a dog person, in writing about these things I find myself thinking about cats and their many lives. I have not counted how many afterlives I have lived since that autumn night in 1989, but I do not think I have yet to reach the magical feline number of nine. But I am accumulating afterlives. In part, I write about cats to try to get a hold on what it has been like to live my life after. Like Nelson, I find myself taking note of both my actual dreams at night as they relate to how I have inhabited the waking world since, and the strange dreaminess of writing, the work I have been doing on this book. I was struck to learn only recently that the dreamlike quality of Maggie Nelson's writing is directly connected to her actual dreams. These less than conscious fears and wishes shape her text. And so it is that *Jane: A Murder* begins with a series of dreams that ask what it could have been like in those last moments of her aunt's life, after she was shot in the head, her skull opened to the light of the moon. In each scenario that Nelson imagines, this light fades, leaving only a hole that aches.

The freckle is turning purple, a miniature contusion. Then darker purple still as the flowers begin to grow heavy with their petals. The leaves flop over the edge and begin to dangle to the floor as the spot begins to blacken.

Ever so slowly, the spot becomes a hole.[9]

For me, life after began as a waking dream, a nightmare. The morning after I was raped, I was unable to get up. I could not awaken from the nightmare of the night before. Only slowly did I realize that it was not a dream.

After a while, after I had become accustomed to this new life, the dream turned into something else. What I experienced then, during this first of what became a series of critical transitions, was a different kind of dream. This is not easy to explain. I moved from that initial experience of life as a waking dream—a nightmare that I could not escape—into a different kind of dream. And this, the second dream, was oddly euphoric and abiding. It lasted for years. The elation, I understood, was a response to the fact that I had not died. It was a response to my profound sense that not only had I not died but I was alive and living the life I longed to live. This dream was a wish fulfillment.

When my life was threatened, I feared that I would not be able to live out my life's dream of becoming a scholar, a teacher, and a writer. This is what I thought about as I was being choked. I had just recently found my academic voice, and the possibility of losing it, of losing the life I longed to live, terrified me. Within months of the rape, I took my doctoral exams. Over the course of the next year, I defended my dissertation proposal, interviewed for the one and only tenure-track job I had applied for, and got the job. By 1993 I had completed my degree and was in the process of securing two book contracts, one for my dissertation and the other for an edited collection of essays. I was living fully the life I had thought I might lose. Even rereading these words now, I feel an energy that makes me read them quickly, breathlessly. This was another afterlife, and it was exhilarating.

This was a different kind of dream. And, over the course of almost twenty years, I basked in the sheer pleasure of having what the singer-songwriter Lucinda Williams describes as "all of this and passionate kisses." This was my life and it was very good. It was so good that during this long, expansive period—almost my entire professional life—I sometimes could hardly believe my good fortune. At those moments, I wondered if perhaps I had in fact died on that November night in 1989. Perhaps my life was but a dream—not a nightmare but a beautiful fantasy, maybe too good to be true. Writing about these experiences is a bit embarrassing. This is not what trauma survivors are supposed to say. But my joy was so vivid and so profound that I cannot describe it without imagining my life as the dream of someone who had died.

The sadness, the loss, the not knowing what my life would or could have been had I not been raped—all this was relegated to the edges of this fantasy. It was a trace of the flip side of my wish fulfillment, connected to the tinge of fear that this life was only a dream. At certain moments, I wondered how I might know for sure that I hadn't died, that I was not already dead. Death was a part of the story, but my focus was on living as fully as I could. It was only as my mother faded that this dreamy life began to unravel. And when she died, the lights went out. Confronted by her death, by the loss of someone I loved fiercely, I was badly shaken. I woke up in a different place.

In the midst of my mother's decline, both before and after her death, I had my own series of recurring dreams, nighttime dreams. Among them was a nightmare that still often wakes me in the middle of the night or early morning hours. In this abiding and familiar dream, my dogs are missing. The dogs in the dream vary; they are often one of my beloved companions—Bleiben, Moses, Walden, or Sam—but the dream is quite consistent. I do not know where the dogs are. I have somehow lost track of them, and I always come to this discovery too late. I begin to panic. I realize that days have gone by since I last saw them. I am afraid I have neglected them, and I worry that they have been harmed. At least since Bleiben, the dog who became my daily companion just after the rape, I can remember having some version of this dream. Bleiben, whose name is the German verb to remain, to survive, to endure, was my orphaned golden retriever. He stayed. His constant companionship allowed me to get on with my life and eventually to live on my own again. The night after the rape, I knew that I could not live alone. I wanted, needed, a dog.

Awakening

During my still euphoric dreamy life, just as I was completing my last book—a book about ghosts and the ways in which different losses touch and intermingle with one another—I met Maggie Nelson. She had just published *Jane: A Murder*. We met at the home of Christina Crosby and Janet Jakobsen in Middletown, Connecticut, where we had both been invited to dinner. This was not long after the bicycle accident that left Christina a quadriplegic, an experience powerfully recounted in her memoir, *A Body Undone*. Nelson is a close friend and former student of Christina's, and at the time was a visiting professor in the English Department at Wesleyan University, where Christina teaches. Janet and I are close friends; she was the person who came with me to the hospital the night I was raped and stood by my side for the duration of my rape exam. It was at this dinner that I first heard Maggie Nelson tell not only the story of her newly published book but also the remarkable, just unfolding tale of how this long cold criminal case was coming back to life.

Nelson had recently returned from Michigan, where she had attended the preliminary hearing in her aunt's murder case. The Michigan State Police had begun an investigation. A DNA match had just been found, more than thirty years later. This extraordinary story would become the basis for Nelson's book *The Red Parts*, a memoir and account of the trial surrounding her aunt's murder. And that memoir would become the inspiration for the book before you now.

Maggie Nelson's description of the courtroom took my breath away. It was there that she saw, for the first time, the clothing her aunt was wearing on the night she was murdered. Although she had spent years researching and writing about her aunt's life and death, Nelson had not, until that moment, seen the array of her aunt's possessions, which had been in police custody. These aging garments were stained with the DNA evidence that brought the case back to life.

It is hard for me to tell this story without gesturing, without carefully holding up my hands, thumb and index finger touching, as if delicately holding those frail pieces of clothing. Hearing this story inspired me to learn more about what happened to the evidence in my own case, my own clothing.

Despite my attachment to objects, to those school shoes and undershirts, in all those years I had not given a second thought to the "evidence" taken from my home the night I was raped. I had not thought about those everyday objects in all that time, and yet hearing about this other woman's clothing sent me on this journey. I became obsessed with questions of evidence. How long are such items held? What are the rules around these practices? How are these objects managed in police storage, and how are they connected to the vast amount of "rescued evidence" held in Holocaust collections, or to all the unprocessed rape kits that remain in limbo?

But I need to say this somewhat differently. Nelson's story was a shock. It was as if I had discovered that I was living out a version of my own recurring nightmare. This time, it was not my dogs who had gone missing; it was my clothing, my linens—the intimate possessions of that little girl who once talked to her shoes and still puts on her shirts upside down and inside out—that had been long lost. How could I possibly have forgotten? When I met Maggie Nelson, it had already been more than fifteen years since I was raped. And not once in that long span of time had I thought about these once familiar objects, the things the police might have taken from my home that night.

I did not know what to make of this story of belated return or its legal ramifications. The case of Nelson's aunt was going to court. By that time, I had long since given up on the law's playing a role in my case. The man who raped me was never found. Despite my best efforts, my vigilance—submitting to a rape exam, giving a statement to the police, remaining on constant alert just in case I might see the rapist on the street, regular calls to the police—my case was never opened, nor did I believe that it was ever closed.[10] Nothing happened. Hearing Nelson's story, I was confused. It pointed to a range of possibilities that I had never considered. What if there had been a DNA match in my case? Was this even possible? Had my rape kit been processed? Was the statute of limitations already up? Where was my evidence?

In all of this I found myself identifying with both Nelson, the writer, and her aunt, the victim. I was both of these women and neither of them. And I didn't know what I wanted; I only knew that I needed to write about these things. How had I forgotten about my clothing for so long? What had happened to those soiled garments or that rape kit?

More than twenty-five years after I was raped, during the winter of 2016 while on vacation in Mexico City, my luggage was lost. For almost five days I was without my clothing, and I was furious. I was beside myself. I wanted my suitcase, my clothing. Strangely, belatedly, I was reliving in a different way my nightmare in real time. But this time the discovery of the loss did not come too late. I was convinced that I was in a position to change what could happen. This time, I would not forget my clothing. I would not lose these items forever. I acted. I expressed my anger and frustration with a ferocity that frightened my beloved. And over the course of those few days, each time I returned to the hotel or awakened from sleep, each time I was brought back to the present of the missing suitcase, I propelled myself into action. With a tremendous compulsion, I made phone call after phone call to Aeroméxico and Delta Airlines in reference to my baggage. I enlisted the hotel's concierge and the staff in the executive suites to help me in these inquires. I went online to check the status of my bag again and again. I was desperate to act, even as my efforts became increasingly pointless. These were the kind of things I could not do immediately after I was raped. Then, I had no control over such matters. And even now I can hardly remember what was taken into custody and what I myself threw away that night. The things that were taken away were never returned. In Mexico, I unwittingly expressed my long dormant rage and frustration. I had never been able to do this before, not even in relation to my missing rape kit. All of those things were long gone. They had vanished, it seems, without a trace.

Traces and Intimacies

After my life was threatened, after I was raped and assaulted, nothing was the same. My life has remained off kilter ever since. The euphoria I described above has been tempered by sadness. And so, lately, as I try to bring the pieces of my story together again, the layers, the many threads, I find myself wondering how we know that this life after, this reality, is not a dream. What ties us to the life we lived before, to the violence that shattered that life, and to this life now? How do we make vivid the fact of that break? How do we know it happened and appreciate its effects? How do we hold on to what happened? How do we do this without allow-ing that violation to take over, even as we carry its often invisible scars? How do we allow for the fact that they remain with us? How do we make them manifest without losing ourselves all over again? I want to suggest that objects and artifacts, buildings and landscapes, the very things that I find myself writing about, can serve this purpose. They offer many of us a palpable sense of continuity. And in this way they remind us that the afterlives of these objects are not simply, in Maggie Nelson's terms, figments of our imagination.[11]

But there is more to the presence of these material artifacts. They not only provide a sense of continuity, offering us tangible proof that we are the same people we were before; they also allow us to make connections to others. Through these often ordinary articles, we connect to other people, especially those who also live their lives after violence, trauma, and profound loss. The intimacy that literary scholar Svetlana Boym and novelist Dubravka Ugrešić write about is often occasioned by material objects and places, the shards of life in the former Eastern Europe, later found in Berlin flea markets or echoed in the exhibition of small ephemeral objects found in the stomach of a once beloved walrus in the Berlin Zoo. This is diasporic intimacy. Or in a different but perhaps related way, these insights tell us something about precious and precarious objects like the striped prisoner uniform held at the USHMM. They provide continuity between then and now, the past and its futures. They also allow us to engage with others. They invite conversation.

Objects facilitate human interaction. Tainted artifacts are oddly compelling. They demand our attention. Like Roland Barthes's punctum, they bristle with life. As witnesses to crimes both large and small, they embody a kind of agency. Their vibrancy is bound to the types of promises I am describing here. They help us continue to tell stories and engage with one another. And in these ways they help us remember pasts even as they enable us to shape different futures. Objects, in this sense, traces of past harms, bridge time and space, connecting past to present, before to after. Their palpable presence then and there, but also here and now, matters. Their continued, albeit fragile, existence in the present interrupts the dreaminess, the frightening, alluring, and untenable notion that life after is after life itself. They remind us that we did not die. And the tasks before us are not only about death but also about living on. They point to our ongoing existence. This is how I have come to experience and understand these things.

A Note on Method

This book is a meditation on the allure of once ordinary artifacts that were brushed by violence: on where they take us and how they become animate, the rites and rituals around them, and the arts of holding that transform them into sacred objects through our tender care. This is not history. The book operates on an associative logic. It offers an idiosyncratic take, a meditation on why we are drawn to particular texts, objects, and practices and how they become meaningful. The book explores these acts of commemoration as ongoing practices and shows how they work.

I use the phrase "not unlike" (and others similar to it) to draw attention to significant juxtapositions of objects, problems, phenomena, and experiences that are often *not* put next to one another and whose likeness may thus at first seem unlikely and may even evoke resistance. Unlike a scientist or a historian who makes arguments about what objects, problems, events, or experiences fit into specific categories and why, my task is more akin to a process of clearing away the frames that might keep a viewer from seeing the connections among unlikely juxtapositions of objects, problems, phenomena, and experiences, with the result that each one may better enhance our understanding of the other(s).

This is difficult epistemological work, because it requires consistent self-reflection and critique of one's assumptions. The work is not only done "out there" in an analytical framework of categories. It requires consistently being aware of the stakes of what one is studying and thinking about.[12]

PART 1

Sacred Texts: The Red Parts

CHAPTER 1

The Allure of Bloody Garments
A Medieval Interlude

Perhaps because I have spent hours sermonizing to students about the sins of the passive voice—how it can obfuscate meaning, deaden vitality, and abandon the task of assigning agency or responsibility—I find the grammar of justice maddening. It's always "rendered," "served," or "done." It always swoops down from on high—from God, from the state—like a bolt of lightning, a flaming sword come to separate the righteous from the wicked in Earth's final hour. It is not, apparently, something we can give to one another, something we can make happen, something we can create together down here in the muck. The problem may also lie in the word itself, as for millennia "justice" has meant both "retribution" and "equality," as if a gaping chasm did not separate the two.

—Maggie Nelson, *The Red Parts*, 113

Maggie Nelson writes that justice always seems to swoop "down from on high—from God, from the state—like a bolt of lightning, a flaming sword come to separate the righteous from the wicked in Earth's final hour." And yet what is the curious role of bloodied material artifacts—soiled clothing, the stuff of mere mortals—in these heavenly proceedings? Can we learn something about this aspect of justice from a series of medieval Jewish liturgical poems and their Christian counterparts? Like me, these texts are haunted by traumatic violence. They speak to the desires surrounding the collection and circulation of actual bloody vestments. Both the veneration of Christian relics and the liturgical commemoration of the blood of Jewish martyrs attest to the power of such mortal remains. By returning to the medieval archive, I want to make explicit how these bloodstained memories and their ultimate resolution form the maddening grammar of even contemporary notions of justice as descending from on high—and how, as such, they make it that much more difficult to make justice happen together "down here in the muck" in response to all kinds of violence.

The *Porphyrion* of God Covered in the Blood of Jewish Martyrs

When I first heard my colleague, the historian Kathy Biddick, describe the medieval Jewish image of the royal purple cloak, the *porphyrion* of God, covered in the blood of Jewish martyrs as a kind of archive, an archive that would be opened and read at the end of days, when justice would be done, I was completely taken with this image.[1] It spoke to me in profound ways, linking my own fascination with bloody garments—the stuff of Holocaust collections and criminal evidence in police storage— to a longer historical lineage. I was compelled by the idea that there was an archival impulse that predates contemporary notions of the relationship between trauma and the archive. I was moved by the idea that bloodstains have always held the promise of being recognized, read, and redressed.

For my colleague, that royal cloak, the *porphyrion* of God, was not only a kind of repository of pain but a ledger to be read at the end of days. It would bring justice to those who died. Following the Jewish historian Israel Jacob Yuval, my colleague linked "the traumatic festal intersections of Pentecost and Shavuot" with a reading of the Mainz memorials in the *Hebrew Chronicles of the Crusades.* That Jewish text, she wrote, commemorates "the Jewish martyrdoms that resulted when the Crusader bands, intent on forced baptism, attacked the Jews of Mainz during the feast of Pentecost/Shavuot."[2]

My friend wrote about this twelfth-century celebration of Pentecost as "a powerful communal event during which local clergy paraded with their parishioners to the cathedral church where they were obligated to make oblations." They wore "special quasi-liturgical royal garments" and participated in "the singing of the hymn, *Te Deum*," an ode to bloodied

Christian martyrs. This hymn is "redolent with the images of processing martyrs robed in white garments washed by the precious blood of Christ."[3]

Yuval also writes about beautiful robes covered in the redemptive blood of martyrs, both Jewish and Christian. As Biddick explains:

> When the Ashkenazi *paytanim* [liturgical poets] subsequently mourned this slaughter [of the Jews of Mainz] in liturgical hymn, they did so by imagining an archival device capable of recording and remembering traumatic events. They drew upon the Midrashic image of the *porphyrion* [royal purple cloak] and attributed to it the capability of precise transcribing: "every drop of blood of Jews killed by Gentiles is recorded in a divine 'ledger' in the form of a scarlet garment." This splattered woven textile, an archive of trauma, reverberates with the words of Isaiah 63:2: "why is thy apparel red, and thy garments like his that treads in the wine press?"[4]

This historical account captured my imagination. I wanted to find myself in a tradition. I wanted to lay claim to this bloody Jewish archive of trauma held in a stained piece of clothing. I wanted to legitimate my own contemporary longings by placing them in this tradition. Not only would this ledger be read at the end of days, but justice would be done for those martyrs by virtue of this record. This was a theological vision of divine justice swooping down from on high that would ultimately set right this suffering, and perhaps even my own.

This redemptive vision was also a profoundly shared promise. It was all made material in a haunting Christian artifact from what Biddick argues was on display during those twelfth-century Pentecostal festivities, the Cloisters Cross.[5] Carved into this sacred object is the figure from Isaiah 63:2 emerging from the "wine press" covered in blood.

In combination, the material cross, the procession singing *Te Deum*, and the medieval Jewish liturgical poems express a longing for justice in the face of terrible violence; all speak to the hope for a belated reckoning. I identified deeply with this medieval longing for justice figured in terms of blood spattered upon once pristine garments, evidence of crimes that God might avenge and rectify.

An Ashkenazi Liturgical Archive: Divine Vengeance

As a Jewish studies scholar of the present concerned about other collections of bloodied clothing, I wondered what that *porphyrion* really had to offer me. What did ancient and medieval texts have to say to those of us working through our own traumatic archives? Was it possible for me to read these texts without either the theological continuity of a royal God, a king who passes divine judgment at the end of days, or the solidity of a nation-state and its laws that might secure a claim to justice? Was there a precedent here that I could lean on? I badly wanted this kind of historical company and legitimacy.

To avenge is to retaliate, to punish, to redress, to even the score, to get revenge, what Maggie Nelson describes as retribution. I turn to this verb because this is what Yuval finds in the writings of Ashkenazi Jewry, visions of redemptive vengeance, a series of revenge fantasies in which justice will be served, the wrongs perpetrated on the Jewish community made right. In many Ashkenazi accounts of retribution, the enemies of the Jews are brutally destroyed. In others they are saved only if and when they come to recognize "the great signs and wonders" that God will give the Jews and, thus moved, "turn to our faith and declare that what they inherited from their fathers was a lie. . . . For all the peoples will turn to the faith of the honored God through the many wonders they will see when the Lord will deliver us from this exile."[6] Join us or die: these are the options.

Considering the "historical conditions" (95) in which this bloody messianic vision emerged, Yuval offers this account of the *porphyrion* of God. While my colleague Kathy Biddick attempts to work through medieval Christians' vengeful approach to the Jews who lived among them, and looks at how the fate of those Jews informed the story of British sovereignty, Yuval offers traces of a longer Jewish legacy.

In a lament for Tisha b'Av composed in the wake of the pogroms of 1096, liturgical poet Kalonymus ben Yehudah wrote:

Drops of my blood are counted one by one
And spray their life-blood on your *porphyrion* [a royal garment
    of crimson]

> He will execute judgment among the nations, filling them with
> corpses. (95)

This is the blood that will avenge. It is a "literal accounting by blood." "Every drop of blood of Jews killed by Gentiles," Yuval explains, "is recorded in a divine 'ledger' in the form of a scarlet garment. The account will be settled—if one can say such a thing—to the last drop of blood" (95). Carefully, meticulously, chillingly, in a way not so different from Shylock's measured pound of flesh, justice is defined as blood for blood. And this is only one of many versions of this figure of the divine ledger in the Ashkenazi archive.[7]

In all of the Ashkenazi texts, "the drops of blood of the martyrs are counted one by one and are sprayed on the garment of God, known as his *porphyrion*, so that it may serve as the corpus delicti to punish the killers on Judgment Day" (96). "Corpus delicti" is a Latin juridical term that identifies "the body of a crime." It is the physical evidence that proves the harm that was done. And yet there is an ambiguity. The term is most often used to point to the body or property that was harmed.[8] "Corpus delicti" blurs the line between these two categories, "the physical object upon which the crime was committed,"[9] and the secondary notion of the evidence brought as proof positive of such harm. It is on the basis of such evidence that justice will be done. This is a more technical account of divine judgment, a vision shared by both Jews and Christians.[10] In Revelation 6:9–11, not unlike the procession on Pentecost that Biddick describes, Christian martyrs are given "white robes" that will hold the evidence of their blood. And their suffering too will be avenged at the end of days when the corpus delicti is brought before God.

Blood Matters

The cry to avenge the martyrs—each and every one of them is a shared motif. For both Christians and Jews, each and every drop of blood matters. Even in early Jewish sources, the royal robe stained with the blood of those who died in God's name stands as testimony that will be heard at the end of days. God will make a judgment and put those responsible to death. And in carrying out this act of vengeance, God will bring redemption to the wronged. This ancient trope is picked up as a "central motif in Ashkenazic liturgical poetry (*piyyut*)" (97), where it becomes what Biddick calls a kind of sartorial archive written in blood. This is how the Jewish historian makes his case for a shared Jewish and Christian legacy of redemptive suffering.

For me, the challenge and the disappointment lie in seeing how swiftly a vision of justice in the face of horrific violence and suffering turns into a revenge fantasy, in which justice is bound inextricably to vengeance, manifesting the contradiction at the heart of justice as Nelson writes about it. Retribution takes over; there is no equality.

The Jewish image of God's bloody cloak builds on a shared language of redemptive suffering where Ashkenazi Jews competed with European Christians in familiar terms. Who suffered the most and thus merits redemption?

The way Yuval writes about these bloody images echoes not only the contradictions Nelson describes but also New Testament scholar Tania Oldenhage's reading of the reception history of Christian Passion narratives after the Holocaust.[11] Addressing the bloody hands of a "we" who are guilty, a community of people who are responsible in the Gospel of Matthew for the death of Jesus, Oldenhage shows how this same figure is revived after the Holocaust. In postwar Germany and France, Matthew and its "we" came also to represent those responsible for the Holocaust. This strange reversal resonates with what we have already seen. By moving away from any simple account of biblical Jews figured as guilty for Jesus's death, Oldenhage too offers contradictions. Jews are both victims and perpetrators, innocent and guilty, as are the various others who then take on the mantle of the collective figure of Jesus/Jews. All of our hands are bloody.

Bloodied bodies continue to pile up. Alongside the redemptive blood of martyrs are the blood-soaked vestiges of divine judgment. The God who avenges Israel's enemy Edom is himself like one who "treads in the wine press" (98). Many medieval Jewish texts cite the same verses from Isaiah 63:1–6 that Kathy Biddick describes as central to *Te Deum*, but in these renderings, when God is asked, "Why is thy apparel red, and thy garments like his that treads in the wine press?," God replies, "I have trodden the wine press alone. . . . I trod them in my anger and trampled them in my wrath; their lifeblood is sprinkled upon my garments, and

I have stained all my raiment" (98). Here, the avenging God is covered in blood. "God is compared to one who treads the winepress trampling the grapes, or the Gentiles," says Yuval; "during the treading, their blood is sprayed on the divine garments, which are stained red" (98). Noting this reversal, Yuval explains, "the blood to be sprayed on his apparel will not be the martyr's, as in the Midrash and the Ashkenazic *piyyutim* but of the Gentiles whom he punishes" (98). Here again the motif is shared, but the evidence tells a very different story. As in the text from Revelation, the drops of blood on God's cloak come to include, or shift to be attributed to, the blood of the nations, the enemies who have harmed God's people and who are rightly punished. Justice becomes only another form of bloody carnage.

The motif of the *porphyrion* and the spilled blood of the martyrs who will be avenged at the end of days appears frequently in "Ashkenazic laments after the persecutions that accompanied the First Crusades (1096)" (99). The Ashkenazi made this vision of vengeance into "a legal event" to be proved on the basis of "solid evidence" (99), the evidence contained in all that blood. "This is the function of the *porphyrion*. The shed blood and its impressions on the divine garment are a legal exhibit, by whose means the guilt of the murderers will be proven. Vengeance is no more than a delayed act of justice, to be performed at Judgment Day" (99).

In the larger context of the Crusades, there is a sense in which both Jews and Christians looked to a kind of redemptive violence for solace. For both, Yuval writes, "Vengeance is understood here as punishment intended to set right the balance of justice" (103). More specifically, he goes on to say that this explains how the Crusaders understood their actions against Jews and Muslims, especially against Jews for having crucified Jesus. Vengeance was "the beginning of deliverance" (103).[12]

Revenge Fantasies and Their Materialization

Whether one agrees with Yuval's provocative conclusions, his text makes clear that vengeance is central to the medieval Jewish vision of divine justice. This is one Jewish legacy of holding on to the material past in the name of divine justice. But, for me, this vision, like so many of those found in the Psalms, is more about a kind of revenge fantasy. This vision of retribution is best understood as fantasy, a necessary imaginative engagement and not something to be actualized. Here I follow literary scholar Sidra Ezrahi's cautionary approach to freighted metaphor.[13] As Ezrahi explains in her reading of Uri Zvi Greenberg's poem "For the Sake of a Mother and Her Son and Jerusalem," for example, "Beneath the apparently benign surfaces of an idea of total homecoming lies the impulse to literalize, the pledge of vengeance, the death wish associated with arrival."[14] For Ezrahi, the challenge is to remember the work of metaphor and the overdetermination in some visions of Zionist homecoming, and to resist a too literal reading of such images.[15] As in the medieval case, Greenberg's fantasy echoes the vision of the Psalms and the desire for divine retribution against the enemies of the Jewish people, in the form of their suffering in perpetuity.[16]

In working through this historical legacy, despite my longing for both company and precedent, I am in many ways left bereft. I cannot reclaim the divine ledger as a way of thinking about justice. The *porphyrion* is not an antecedent for my living memory, or even a belated messianic vision of justice. I cannot redeem the medieval Ashkenazic archive of pain. I came to its texts wanting to imagine this evidence, these stories of loss and pain retold at the end of days, as a way of making right the suffering I see all around me in the present. I wanted to see these texts as a promise for a kind of justice to be done for those who died then and there, and perhaps also for those who continue to suffer and die. And, in many ways, they are just that. But vengeance is not what I am looking for. I do not want more blood. My own vision of justice is far from the ways in which this trope and these figures were taken up in the medieval sources that medieval historians read so powerfully. This is not a tradition that I want to hold on to, certainly not in these terms.

In the aftermath of the destruction wrought by crusader bands during the festival of Shavuot, Jews mourned the slaughter in a liturgical hymn. Biddick tells us that "they did so by imagining an archival device capable of recording and remembering traumatic events," a textile archive, "a divine ledger in the form of a scarlet garment."[17] Her account of this garment resonated with my own interest in the literal bloody garments held in police storage and in the Holocaust collections that captured my imagination. And yet, having worked through all of these materials, I am disappointed, again, by what I have found. Vengeance is not what I was hoping for. Like Nelson, I cannot abide by a vision of justice from on high, nor can I wait until the end of days.

The Light of Justice

And so I want to return to that bloody cloak of God and ask what it might mean to read the "divine ledger" in the name of cohabitation and remembrance, as Kathy Biddick imagines it now. But I also want to be able to assign agency and responsibility, as Maggie Nelson suggests. I want to imagine a form of justice performed by us mere mortals down here in the muck as we work through our own bloody ledgers. And I want to make clear that like our medieval ancestors, we too continue to be drawn to these forms of material evidence. Such objects continue to speak to our desires for justice.

Let me try to say this differently. Although it is too often figured in messianic terms, as the separation of "the righteous from the wicked in Earth's final hour," perhaps the magic is closer to hand. The material traces of the violence done to us may themselves hold the key to a more partial reckoning.

Returning to this question in her book *Make and Let Die*, Biddick asks us to imagine a different kind of messianism. She attributes to the medieval Ashkenazi rabbis a strangely contemporary vision infused with a this-worldly magic. The "rabbis imagined the messianic, not so much as a radically different temporal register, but, like quantum physicists, more so as an entangled register of light. Their experience of 'to make die' criss-crossed on the *porphyrion* with 'to let live' in quantum patterns. In contemporary terms, we can think of their messianic *porphyrion* as an infrared apparatus whose spectrum would become visible in the light of justice."[18] In the light of justice, we see both "retribution" and "equality"—"to make die" and "to let live." Under the right conditions, the evidence can be seen and read as a pattern of light. Here, the *porphyrion* becomes for Biddick a lot like Paul Klee's *Angelus Novus*, the inspiration for Walter Benjamin's own this-worldly messianism. But in Biddick's rendering, the image is more concrete. The archival-based oil-transfer process that Klee used to create his angel echoes the medieval bloody cloak. The traces that are reproduced and made visible in Klee's transfer operation are akin to seeing each drop of blood on a textile archive of pain. This is a kind of "quantum vision." Like Freud's "magic writing pad," the oil-transfer process "embodied the disjuncture of inscriptional technologies, their disjointed temporalities, and the supplement of color washes, just as did the 'blood transfer process' into the messianic envisioned by Ashkenazi rabbis."[19] Although I am not particularly interested in reclaiming medieval Jewish messianism, I am moved by how this quantum vision echoes more quotidian contemporary practices. Writing about the strange, belated revival of her aunt's long dormant murder investigation, which ended up hinging on DNA evidence from the victim's clothing, Maggie Nelson asks us to consider what becomes visible under the right light. "If preserved well these bodily traces can last—and remain identifiable—for decades. For millennia, even longer. *DNA is robust*, an analyst explains on the stand. *It can be lost, but it cannot be changed.* Because there is currently no way to date DNA, under the right light, cells from thousands of years ago would glow right alongside the cells we are leaving in our wake today. Under the right light, the present and the past are indistinguishable."[20]

Perhaps like the Klee painting, God's *porphyrion* can be read at a later moment. Perhaps it can be reinvented and reimagined again and again. But the question of what to do with all of this evidence is what matters most to me. Like Kathy Biddick and Maggie Nelson, I want to learn how we can live together without losing sight of our violent legacies.[21] And like Nelson, who fiercely refuses the legitimacy of state violence, I do not want our reckoning with violence to result in more violence.[22]

Being heard, acknowledged, recognized, seen, understood—these are all variations on what it might mean to do justice to those who suffer. There is no epiphany, no moment when everything comes together and the situation is resolved. That too is a fantasy. In the everyday world, this work does not follow a linear trajectory. There is no resolution. There are only various forms of partial reckoning, more harms, and sometimes the suffering is acknowledged not by God or by the state but by other human beings. What draws so many of us to the shards of broken lives is perhaps a kind of recognition, a sense that acknowledgment matters. This is what is possible down here in the muck. And this is what keeps me going.

CHAPTER 2

In the Poet's Hand
The Red Parts

What I do know is this (and here I speak, of course, only for myself): there is no saving thought (*think how your ____ will feel; count your blessings; tomorrow is another day*; etc.) that is ultimately sustaining, no line of poetry, no holy book, no hotline.

—Maggie Nelson, *The Red Parts*, 88–89

Just as I turned off the light in my bedroom, I was attacked. Fighting for my life, I entered a world marked by the memory of trauma and the struggle to survive. Only months after I was raped, I tried to write about what had happened, trying to interrupt the silence all around me. And in the opening pages of that essay, I described my experience.

Years later, returning to that text, I notice that I wrote down the date, November 7, 1989. I am startled by this. When did I begin to think of the date as the first Tuesday in November, an off-year election day? I had forgotten that I ever knew the date, but I had known it then. This is part of what I wrote:

A young man broke into my apartment while I was watching TV. I heard virtually nothing, no more than the regular sounds of wind against the door, the windows and the shade. Nevertheless, he had entered my home. As a woman living alone, I have always been fearful of sounds in the night and I often check to be sure that

I am not just hearing things. This time, I waited a few minutes and then began to look around—just in case. . . . He hid among the shadows. As I breathed a sigh of relief turning off the light in my bedroom, having checked the bathroom (behind the shower curtain), the study, and finally my bedroom (the closet), he jumped out and attacked me.

I can hardly make myself retype my own words, the words I wrote then. But here is the terrible heart of the story:

I screamed and I pleaded. I tried to bargain with my attacker. I offered him money, please not to hurt me. His words to me, his first and most chilling words, "Give me some pussy. Give it to me." He wanted me. Not me as a person. . . . No, he wanted my body, the body of any woman. He wanted a "pussy." And he was violently and aggressively taking, as if it was his to take.

I fought back. I yelled and screamed which only served to provoke his anger and his rage against me. He began to choke me. He told me he would kill me as he tightened his grip around my neck. He meant it. I nearly passed out. After what seemed like an eternity of struggle, of escalating threats and violent beating, I stopped fighting for control of my body and concentrated on saving my life. I did not choose to be raped. I struggled to live. I took off my pants while he kept a tight hold on my neck. He threw me on the bed and raped me.[1]

I took off my pants—the rest fades. It was a decision without a choice. I hate this memory.

Circling back to the early days after I was raped, I remember a glimmer of hope. In those first weeks and months, I held on tightly to the story of another woman in my graduate program. She had been raped not long before I arrived. She was an ordained minister who had served in a congregation in downtown Atlanta. As I remember it, she was raped in the church. Not only had she survived, but some months later she saw the rapist on the street, and this led to his apprehension. There was a trial and he was convicted and sent to jail.

But her story was not my story. Despite my vigilance, I never found the man who raped me.

In June 2014, I made a formal open-records request for information about the evidence in my case. I wanted to know what had happened to my sheets, my clothing, and my rape kit. I waited months for a reply. My interactions with the police had given me no confidence that any evidence had been saved, but I needed to be sure. After waiting all summer for a response to my request, I finally called the Atlanta police in the fall. I was handed off to many different people but eventually was transferred to a sergeant in the sex crimes division. She told me that she had my case file on her desk. I had not even thought to ask about the file because I had assumed that it no longer existed and that my story had vanished from the public record. At that time, records were not digitized. She and her partner were looking for my evidence. Although they never were able to locate it, she was patient and answered my questions. When I got off the phone, I realized that I had failed to ask for my case file. I emailed her and she sent me a PDF of the file.

It was not until the fall of 2018 that I was able to recognize that among the documents in my case file was a "Supplementary Offense Report," form 32-D-101. The officer in charge of my case wrote, "My investigation has not produced evidence to identify a suspect in this case. At this time until any new leads or evidence are discovered, I'm placing this case on an inactive status." The report was dated January 21, 1990. Two months after I was raped, the case went cold. It has never warmed—a pair of sweatpants still on the floor.

Wait, I was wrong. I had seen this file. And I had even written about this recovery. I wrote about my belated longing for my clothing, my sweatpants. I also wrote about the shock of seeing my own face in the file, a victim mug shot that I did not remember was taken that night I was raped. I wrote about not being able to reproduce that image. I had no recollection of any of the other photographs in the file.

Four years later, among these documents of which I now had partial custody, I saw for the first time what I had not remembered: a photograph of my sweatpants (fig. 3). The sweatpants are my connection, the thin thread that brings me back to tell the story differently. I ache for

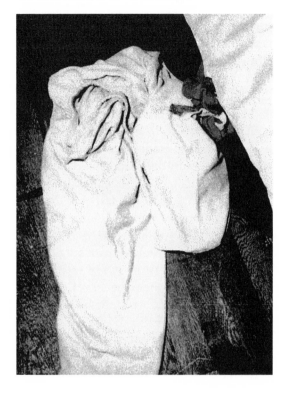

Fig. 3. Sweatpants. Photo: author.

those pants. Seeing them there in a heap on the floor next to my bed hurls me back to that terrible moment.

"No line of poetry, no holy book, no hotline"—I have learned lessons of partial reckoning from Maggie Nelson. In her prose and poetry, I have found companionship and meaning when neither God nor secular justice could reach me. Nelson takes up the cold case of her aunt, Jane Mixer, dead for decades, murdered when she was a student at the University of Michigan Law School, years before Maggie was born. In *Jane: A Murder*, Nelson, who reminded her family of her aunt Jane, tracks what happened through scraps of evidence in newspapers, footage of television coverage, police files, Jane's diaries, and memories of those who knew Jane Mixer.

When Nelson was completing the book, there was a break in this thirty-five-year-old case, a DNA match. Her response to this discovery became her memoir, *The Red Parts*. It opens with the strange coincidences that mark this tale of murder and belated justice. As the cover copy on the original edition explains, "In an instance of remarkable serendipity, more than three decades later, a 2004 DNA match led to the arrest of a new suspect in Jane's murder at precisely the same time that Nelson was set to publish a book of poetry about her aunt's life and death—a book she had been working on for years, and which assumed her aunt's case to be closed forever. The Red Parts chronicles the uncanny series of events that led to Nelson's interest in her aunt's death, the reopening of the case, the bizarre and brutal trial that ensued, and the effects these events had on the disparate group of people they brought together."[2] Nelson's account motivated me to tell my own story.

Reading her books and tracing her struggle to reckon with this chain of events, I begin to come to terms with my own losses. In the poet's hand, ordinary objects—in her aunt's case, a raincoat, a tampon, and a towel, like my sweatpants—are transformed into talismans, offering a different form of doing justice and living on. Hers is not an easy tale to tell, but she shows that it is possible to write our way into a different place. She made room for me to figure out how to continue living and writing and loving in a new intellectual space.

As I noted in the introduction, I had met Nelson through mutual friends not long after the preliminary hearing for what became her aunt's murder trial, and that meeting is what led me to write this book. Over dinner, she explained what it had been like to sit in that Michigan courtroom, having lived so long with the shards of her aunt's life, interviews with those closest to her, her fiancé, her mother and grandfather. Most important was what Maggie Nelson found in her aunt's many journals and diaries. Her aunt's voice lies at the heart of *Jane: A Murder*. As I read *The Red Parts*, visceral descriptions of the material evidence, like the clothing that her aunt wore the night she was murdered, set my story back in motion.

As Nelson tried to make sense of this loss, she challenged the longing for redemption, including the longing expressed in the contemporary Jewish and Christian texts that I was studying at Emory in 1989, at the time of my rape. She ultimately shunned her own religious tradition and its promises of redemptive suffering, of bloody salvation (the body and blood of Christ).[3] Like Nelson, I had turned away from the religious traditions I was studying and the one in which I was raised. Disappointed by both God and the law, I found my work changing.

Seeing Red: Veins and Verses

Rereading *The Red Parts*, I repeatedly found myself trying to trace the threads through pages of messy annotations and highlighted passages. And then there are my notes on my notes. I wanted to understand. I wanted to enter into the logic of the text and discover what it could show me. I longed for revelation, even knowing that there are no answers. I am dogged, a hound on the scent of the missing evidence.

A part of me has loved losing myself in this text. Distracted by the intricacies of my search, I forget that I am trying to figure out how to tell my own story. Where do I add my voice? How do I justify this conversation? And how might attending to a telling detail help me get to a different place?

Nelson's text folds in on itself again and again, in echoes, iterations, formal connections. Many of the figures are strangely intertwined: boyfriends, husbands, fathers, grandfathers, sisters and mothers, mothers and daughters, murderers and victims. I am less interested in retracing these connections than in unraveling the threads that hold the text together. And I am now fearful that my own musings are simply new iterations of the books and articles I have already written. Is the story line different? If I can figure out what Nelson is doing, perhaps I can do it myself.

I took off my pants, a choiceless choice.[4] He was choking me. This is what it was like for me to approach my own original state of breakdown, though I did not die and I had no trial. I am not Maggie Nelson, and I am not Jane Mixer.

There is no saving discourse. Nelson hates clichés. She wants but then refuses easy answers and demands that her readers do the same. She does not want this story to be confused with other stories, all those tales we think we already know that have been repaired through such narration.

I struggle to understand how to write my own story without such clichés. And I reach back to that original moment of breakdown. I return to the night I was raped, and those sweatpants. This is the terrible story that I continue to reach toward. I both lost and saved my life that night. My life after was and is different, both lost and found.[5] Part of what I lost was my faith in God and the state.

In my first book, *Jews and Feminism: The Ambivalent Search for Home*, I catch a glimpse of what I lost. I had left my parents' Jewish home to study religion at Emory. "I let go of my father's rational and highly secular vision of the world," even as I held tight to "his faith in liberalism and the promise of America."[6] As I explained it then, "The liberal values he had taught me as being American and Jewish I made into a religious faith." I "theologized his position as my own." The passage continues, and here I find a trace, a small glimpse, of who I was before, what I had believed. "God was not so much a part of my father's view of the world; theology was my innovation. I needed the power of such claims to escape certain vulnerabilities, and religious faith gave me some security. I needed to ground my values in something more firm than what my father had given me" (23). In the odd alchemy of my American Jewish identity, what I lost was my faith in both God and the state. I had imagined these situating commitments as safe dwelling places, the legacies of my various inheritances, Jewish and liberal, each a kind of home. There was, in fact, no home. I could no longer imagine escaping my vulnerability. I had no recourse to a form of justice, either local or transcendent.

I wrote about the sadness that washed over me as I wrote those words. I wasn't sure then whether it was harder for me or for my parents. I suspect that I was hiding behind them, praying perhaps that they could still offer me shelter. But the grief was mine. After I had given up on answers, Nelson gave me a language for living without certitude.

Despite my commitment to theology, I had not escaped "certain vulnerabilities." Religious faith no longer offered me a place to "ground my values." Writing about this break and the kind of letting go it precipitated, I explained in *Jews and Feminism*, "This is a book about passionate embraces. It is about the interplay between the need to hold on and the need to let go of the places, relationships, and traditions we call home.

It is about the delicacy of all such attachments and the ways we have come to make them seem lasting" (xiii). My attachment to all that I had believed in loosened. I had already entered into a different life, an afterlife. I was learning to live with uncertainty. I was trying to imagine a different relationship to these once seemingly sturdy commitments. I am still entangled in these struggles—of holding on and letting go. In this afterlife, I have no saving thoughts.

I cannot stay away from Nelson. I keep reminding myself that this is my story, but her companionship helps me find my way.

Making notes in that Michigan courtroom on yellow legal pads, Nelson writes letters to her estranged lover that she will never send. She will "describe each of the autopsy photos in detail," imagining them for him as if "only he can understand their burden, their horror."[7] She hears from him only once. She had imagined him by her side for the duration of the trial, but he is already in his own, different story. By writing about the pieces of evidence, even if she never sends the letters, she keeps her focus. She begins to tell a different story. And so, each night, in the only place where she can be alone—the shower—she writes:

> I will get down on my knees and weep, letting the water run over my body, praying to get better, praying not to hurt myself any more than I'm already hurting, praying that this loss, that this whole time, will move over me, through me, like a dark storm passing over a great plain. A great plain which is, essentially, my soul. A soul which is neither light nor dark, neither wholly alone nor wholly with any other, certainly not with God, just flat, open, deathless, and free. Curled up in a wet ball on the tile floor I will hear myself say, *Something in me is dying*. I no longer know to whom I am talking.[8]

She wants to be like the Buddha and train in the fire of antiviolence activists, "'master warriors'—*not warriors who kill and harm but warriors of nonaggression who hear the cries of the world. . . .[Men] and women who are willing to train in the middle of the fire . . . [men and women who] enter challenging situations in order to alleviate suffering.*"[9] She struggles to hold on.

As she settles into the trial, the combination of her thwarted desire and her strong sense of hitting rock bottom conspire to make the shower, its own kind of baptismal prayer, a ritual act of dying to be reborn.[10] Reading these Christian tropes, I find a kind of release from my own tradition. Nelson shows me how to hold on and let go, all at the same time.

I initially wrote about what it meant for me not to share the photographs taken of me the night I was raped.[11] I did not want those images to circulate. I wanted to control what was or was not said about them. Even now, I am still reaching for D. W. Winnicott's "original state of breakdown."[12] Arrested by the terror on my own face, even three decades later, I was unable to see what I thought I was looking for when I opened the file. I did not see the photograph of my sweatpants. I need to understand how I missed this.

A photograph, *Photo #3*: a close-up image of the entry wound. "When detectives arrive at the scene of a homicide," Nelson writes, "they start far away from the body, and move slowly in towards it, so as not to disturb anything, taking photographs, collecting evidence in sweeping, concentric circles."[13] Nelson's prose echoes this nested methodical engagement, circling around Jane's body from different angles, homing in on the physical evidence at the heart of the state's case. This circling pattern also marks my slow journey back to the evidence that was collected and the testimony I gave to the Atlanta police, the material collected in my case file, and the evidence I found in my own writing. This is how I was able slowly to circle back to those sweatpants.

Justice

What is justice?[14] Why spend all that time in the courtroom? These are the questions that disturb Nelson as she considers what it meant for her to witness the trial of her aunt's murderer. In chapter 12 of *The Red Parts*, "After Justice," she wrestles with these questions. She asks us to consider the chasm between the practices of the courtroom, the realm of the law, and the elusive goal of achieving justice. She is troubled by the challenges of what it means to be a subject before the law, to seek, to rush after justice. She wrestles with the tension between retribution and fairness. In the case of her aunt, Jane Mixer, the process of finding "justice" is belated and protracted, occurring thirty-six years after the crime. Is it really justice?

My story follows an inverted logic of its own. What I discovered belatedly, almost thirty years later, was that my case was open for only a moment before it was closed. I learned from the detective in sex crimes that in the early 2000s, the Atlanta police did revisit cold cases of rape and murder from as far back as the 1980s in response to advances in DNA analysis. Yet I know nothing about what happened to my rape kit or those sweatpants. There is no documentation. And the evidence itself cannot be located.

Once upon a time, I studied Jewish and Christian theology, looking for answers. But after I was raped, I found myself, like Maggie Nelson, unable to continue that quest. I discovered that "there is no saving thought . . . that is ultimately sustaining."[15] There are aches that have no remedy. I know them in my own body. But I also know that fierce and honest writing makes it possible for me to carry on. I have evidence, the image of those sweatpants in a pile on the floor. They speak to the horror of that night, to the terror of that choiceless choice to save my life. In this afterlife, I hold fast to Nelson's words so that I do not have to experience my pain alone.

CHAPTER 3

In the Potter's Hands
Containers of Loss

It is not just things that carry stories with them. Stories are a kind of thing, too. Stories and objects share something, a patina. I thought I had this clear, two years ago before I started, but I am no longer sure how this works. Perhaps patina is a process of rubbing back so that the essential is revealed, the way that a striated stone tumbled in a river feels irreducible, the way that this netsuke of a fox has become little more than a memory of a nose and a tail. But it also seems additive, in the way that a piece of oak furniture gains over years and years of polishing.

—**Edmund de Waal, *The Hare with Amber Eyes*, 349**

A world-renowned potter, Edmund de Waal suggests that things and stories share a materiality. Repeated touch and critical engagement leave their mark. Objects, both worn and pristine, offer tactile access to otherwise often inaccessible pasts. A patina is a green film formed naturally on copper or bronze by long exposure to light or chemicals. It is, as *Merriam-Webster's* explains, "valued aesthetically for its color." More broadly construed, it is "a surface appearance of something grown beautiful with age or use." A less common definition suggests that it can refer to "an appearance or aura that is derived from association, habit, or established character." For de Waal, both texts and objects are made beautiful through repeated handling. As a potter and a crafter of stories, he appreciates the give-and-take that marks the making and the circulation of objects that carry stories, and of stories as things.

Through a single salvaged collection of 264 netsukes, small carved Japanese sculptures, de Waal crafts his family's story. In *The Hare with Amber Eyes*, he writes about his family's banking empire and all of their holdings, a world of wealth populated by precious cultural and artistic works—books, paintings, sculptures, rugs, furniture. All of this was carefully documented, inventoried, packaged up, and taken away by the Nazis. The tiny Japanese sculpture collection is what is left of this once powerful family's valuable possessions. The "hare with amber eyes" refers to one of his favorites.

The recovery of even this small piece of the family's fortune was not adjudicated by the law. Nor was it an act of religious redemption. The return of this collection is a different kind of doing justice, an unexpected act of love and loyalty—each netsuke a token of that affection. By telling their story, de Waal's book holds the pain and sorrow of his family's Holocaust story. *The Hare with Amber Eyes* is a "container that can hold all of the brokenness, and make it beautiful."[1]

The handmade and handheld quality of de Waal's ceramic pieces in particular speaks to me. Haptic images saturate his prose, reminding me of my most precious and troubling possessions relating to my rape. The potter I was falling in love with in 1989 gave me bowls, dishes, small vessels—objects both practical and beautiful. Often rough to the touch, these earthenware containers have held my pain and my brokenness with delicacy.

I had been introduced to my potter early that fall; we had only been together a couple of months before I was attacked. We had mutual friends. He was a doctoral student in psychology. Having completed his course work, he spent most days making pottery in a studio on the grounds of a former Coca-Cola mansion. He was applying for clinical internships. The pots were there from the very beginning of our acquaintance, and my relationship to him and to the objects he made only deepened after I was raped.

In the Potter's Hands

All of this matters because my job is to make things. How objects get handled, used and handed on is not just a mildly interesting question to me. It is *my* question. I have made many, many thousands of pots. I am very bad at names, I mumble and fudge, but I am good on pots. I can remember the weight and the balance of a pot, and how its surface works with its volume. I can read how an edge creates tension or loses it. I can feel if it has been made at speed or with diligence. If it has warmth.

—Edmund de Waal, *The Hare with Amber Eyes*, 16

Although the pieces of de Waal's netsuke collection are not themselves bloody or broken, they carry the weight of his family's profound loss and tell that family's story. De Waal knows and cares about objects. He opens his volume with a long passage from Proust's protagonist Charles Swann. In a passage from *Cities of the Plain*, Swann speaks eloquently of our intimate relationship with things. "Even when one is no longer attached to things, it's still something to have been attached to them; because it was always for a reason which other people did not grasp." De Waal invokes the "mania of all collectors," whose passion is a kind of collection of love affairs about which the world knows little. His text pays homage to a family legacy of collecting. He writes about the pleasure and allure of so many precious objects, a vast collection forcibly winnowed down. He tells the story through his passion for the singular collection that remains.

In lush prose that belies de Waal's reticence about names and words, this material artist is also a careful crafter of narrative: "how objects are handed on is all about story-telling."[2] He suggests some of the various motives behind the exchange of precious objects: "Because I love you. Or because it was given to me. Because I bought it somewhere special. Because you will care for it. Because it will complicate your life. Because it will make someone else envious" (17). But having suggested these reasons, he continues, "There is no easy story in legacy. What is remembered and what is forgotten? There can be a chain of forgetting, the rubbing away of previous ownership as much as the slow accretion of stories" (17). This is how this potter begins his story. For de Waal, the patina, the slow accretion of stories, the building up of a vessel, are most salient. In the end, he asks, "What is being passed on to me with all of these small Japanese objects?" (17). And so this astonishing story of so many love affairs, so many precious and beloved objects, begins in the potter's hands.

The figure of "the potter's hand," of course, has wider resonance. The biblical text of Jeremiah 18:1–11 comes to mind. As a scholar of religion, I can hardly avoid associations with sacred texts. And yet, looking more closely at the biblical figure of the potter, I want to show the contrast between de Waal's notion of the potter's ethics—what attracts me to the promise of being held in a potter's hands—and the prophet's cautionary tale. The biblical story is a provocation. It echoes in a different way some of the ambivalence of my own story of a lost love and its remains.

Like mine, de Waal's relationship to the biblical tradition is complicated. His Jewish family's story has very little to do with Hebrew scripture. The Ephrussi family becomes both Christian and Buddhist over time, converting after the war. This cosmopolitan European Jewish family had already, by the time of the Anschluss, distanced itself from formal commitments to Jewish faith and practice.

The Biblical Potter, Turning Away

De Waal knows that his family was Jewish, though their religious practice decidedly is not. As a child, his grandmother desired "rabbinic instruction." The family's Jewishness is also expressed in his great uncle's wish to join his father and "all of his friends, his Jewish friends," at the Wiener Club on Thursday evenings (9). Iggie, the last of the Ephrussi children, died in Japan and was buried in a Buddhist grave next to his long-time companion. In their home, in his companion's quarters, there was, de Waal explains, "a little shrine bearing photographs of his mother and Iggie's mother, Emmy, where prayers were said and the bell was rung" (8). At Iggie's funeral, after de Waal cannot remember the right Japanese words to recite in his great uncle's memory, he recalls Iggie as a Jew. Although "Iggie is given his new Buddhist name, his *kaimyo*, to help him in his next life," he is mourned as a Jew alongside his parents and his siblings. "In this room in this Buddhist temple in this Tokyo suburb," de Waal writes, "I say the Kaddish for Ignace von Ephrussi who is so far from Vienna, for his father and his mother, and for his brother and sister in their diaspora" (10).

Mourning is a site of Jewish memory for de Waal. He returns to the Kaddish at the end of the book in the context of his grandmother's death. At her funeral, his father recites the Kaddish for his mother, Elisabeth.

She had been given that "rabbinic instruction," but she only mentioned this fact in her nineties: "I asked my father for permission. He was surprised" (347). And so, when his grandmother died two years later, de Waal explains, "my father, the clergyman in the Church of England, born in Amsterdam with a childhood everywhere in Europe, stood in his Benedictine-black, rabbinical-black cassock and recited the Kaddish for his mother in the parish church near her nursing home" (347–48). De Waal also writes toward the end of his prologue, "I know that my family were Jewish, of course, and I knew they were staggeringly rich, but I really don't want to get into the sepia saga business, writing up some elegiac Mitteleuropa narrative of loss" (15). The important point here is that he owns that they were Jewish and he is not sentimental.

I mention this family's complicated relationship to Jewish tradition as a way back into my own messy connections to the figure of the potter and my work in religious studies. I decided to call this chapter "In the Potter's Hands" long before I realized that I had invoked a biblical figure. Only when my beloved reminded me of this connection did I find myself, once again, in the company of sacred texts. Confronted by the resonances between my appreciation for "the hands of the potter" and its biblical antecedent, I opened the pages of my Tanakh, my sacred text. I suspect that I was still looking for something more solid to hold on to, a lingering hope for some theological security. What did the figure of the potter's hands mean to me? How does this figure ultimately differ from the prophetic vision in Jeremiah 18:1–11? To answer these questions, I needed to explain what I found in the biblical text. I wanted scripture to affirm my attraction to the promise of the potter and his creations. But this is not what the text offers.

Chapter 18 of the book of Jeremiah begins with God's call to the prophet to go to the house of the potter, where he will hear God's word. Jeremiah finds the potter at work at his wheels (18:3). "And if the vessel that he was making was spoiled, as happens to clay in the potter's hand, he would make it into another vessel, such as the potter saw fit to make" (18:4).[3] The potter finds a flaw in what he is making. He feels it in his hands and, based on that intimate knowledge, he starts again. Using the same clay, he makes a vessel that he deems viable. This echoes de Waal's concept of the potter's ethics, which he learned in Japan and wrote about in an article titled "Japan and the Potter's Ethic: Cultivating a Reverence for Your Materials and the Marks of Age" (3). As a devotee of the English potter Bernard Leach, de Waal had already learned, well before going to Japan, "about respect for the material and about fitness for purpose" (2).

In Jeremiah, the potter explains God's own work as the maker of human beings. This account builds on the nexus of meanings in the Hebrew word *yotzer*, "potter," which comes from the root *yatzar*, to form, fashion, or create.[4] Jeremiah 18 makes clear that God the potter and creator can also be the destroyer of whole peoples and communities. His decision hinges on the notion of what he judges "fit" or "good." Unlike the kind of delicacy that de Waal describes, God the potter makes this assessment into a moral judgment and in fact a threat. "O house of Israel, can I not deal with you like this potter? says the Lord. Just like clay in the hands of the potter, so are you in My hands, O house of Israel" (18:6).

Not only is the house of Israel in God's hands, as a lump of clay on the potter's wheel, the text continues, but "at one moment I may decree that a nation or a kingdom shall be uprooted and pulled down and destroyed" (18:7). The Lord can make and break a nation at will. And in the next verses, the prophet makes explicit God's judgment. In Jeremiah 18:8, the term used for human transgression is "wickedness," in some translations, "evil." If the people turn from their evil ways, God will build them up, but if they engage in wicked deeds, he will punish them accordingly. "But if that nation against which I made the decree turns its back from its wickedness, I change My mind concerning the punishment I planned to bring on it" (18:9). And in the next verse the choice is made even clearer: "but if it does what is displeasing to Me and does not obey Me, then I change My mind concerning the good I planned to bestow upon it" (18:10).

In the New Revised Standard Version, the text is more explicit still: "But if it does evil in my sight, not listening to my voice, then I will change my mind about the good that I had intended to do to it." The narrative ends in verse 18:11, where Jeremiah addresses the people of Judah and the inhabitants of Jerusalem, saying, "And now, say the men of Judah and the inhabitants of Jerusalem: Thus, said the Lord: I am devising disaster for you and laying plans against you. Turn back, each of you, from your wicked ways, and mend your ways and your actions!"[5]

In this verse, the divine potter demands something of his clay. He can, in the NRSV translation, "shape evil against you." The clay or the people can behave and make amends, or else. The rest of the chapter is about Israel's failings and the people's need to repent, echoing other prophetic texts that feminize "Maiden Israel" as a wayward wife.[6] Of course, the prophetic text is intended as a powerful warning that the people must change their ways, but in this brief instance I am more interested in the tension between the actual labor of the potter, a craftsman who sensitively engages with his materials, and the judging God. The potter makes vessels designed to withstand the wear and tear of everyday life, not to mention the fire of the kiln. This statement is not about moral judgment; the point is that the firing itself is a kind of test, and that by extending the metaphor in reverse, we can see that the clay pots, like the men of Judah and the inhabitants of Jerusalem or even the maiden Israel, all have some agency. But I am not convinced.

Despite my deployment of the figure of the potter, the biblical text does not begin to capture the kind of tender tactile experience that I associate with being in a potter's hands. For me, Jeremiah 18 is not about justice from on high. To speak of being "in the potter's hands" is not merely to use an allegory. The prophetic text does not convey what de Waal is doing in his memoir. Nor does it begin to explain my experience with my own potter. These artists not only offer tender regard, a knowing touch; they quite literally make objects that are both beautiful and useful.

As a scholar of religion seeking a precedent, hoping against hope that there might be something of use to me in this sacred text, I am disappointed in Jeremiah. In this instance, to be, in a biblical sense, "in the potter's hands" is to be vulnerable. Flaws are figured as moral failings and the clay itself is called to task, blamed for whatever goes wrong. What disturbs me in the context of de Waal's work and my own story is that the application of this prophetic logic becomes a form of victim blaming. Blaming the victim offers control, but at a high cost. If only I had double-checked the back door of my apartment, if only I had run out of the house when I first heard a strange noise, I could have prevented my rape. This is not helpful thinking, and although it is part of a certain brand of Haredi Judaism—ultra-Orthodox Holocaust thought—it is a stance I reject fiercely. The theological position that the victim is to blame for what befalls her assumes that the trial by fire that was the Holocaust was about the moral failings of the Jewish people. The Shoah becomes punishment for not following Jewish law, for not practicing Judaism correctly.[7] It blames victims like the members of de Waal's family for their fate. I reject this view, among many other judgments from on high. I much prefer to put my faith in the power of the actual potter and the work of his hands.

In de Waal's work, the human potter and his touch, his sensitive hold, are all about love for the object and its maintenance. This protective tenderness is paramount. In other words, although the potter must figure out the viability of what is in his hands—any given pot—he does so not in order to punish the clay but rather to make sure that this particular form, the vessel before him, is viable. He decides whether it will withstand the heat of the kiln and come out the other side of the firing something both beautiful and utilitarian, a vessel fit for human use. And given the proximity in everyday life between such objects and those who use them, there is an affective engagement between the vessel and its user that also demands our attention. There is a tenderness between handled objects and those who use them. As affect theorist Sara Ahmed explains, this may be especially true when addressing objects as fragile as those made of clay, objects that can easily shatter.[8]

Vitrines and the Holding of Objects

De Waal quotes Proust's Swann in the epigraph to *The Hare with Amber Eyes*: "I open my heart to myself like a sort of vitrine, and examine one by one all those love affairs of which the world can know nothing." A vitrine, *Merriam-Webster's* tells us, is a "glass showcase or cabinet especially for displaying fine wares or specimens." This display case takes its name from the French, "*vitre*, a pane of glass, from Old French, from Latin *vitrum*." Its first known use seems to have been around the very moment when the Ephrussi family were collecting such wares in Paris.[9] Family stories from the 1880s are recounted in the opening chapters of *The Hare with Amber Eyes*. De Waal's story begins and ends with vitrines that hold the netsuke collection that is passed down to him.

This collection is venerated and displayed, kept safe and visible—and accessible.[10] In the final chapter, he writes, "The collection's latest resting-place is in London. The Victoria and Albert Museum is getting rid of some of its old vitrines to make way for new displays. I buy one" (349). De Waal describes the great effort involved in installing this vitrine in his family home and the great pleasure of giving back to his children the experiences of his grandmother and her siblings, who grew up with this collection. His children have access to the astonishing treasures. "It is seven feet high on its mahogany base and is made of bronze. It has three glass shelves" (350). As he affixes this vitrine to his walls, de Waal recalls his own childhood collections and the vitrine that housed them. He has reclaimed a decommissioned container and put it to new use: "When I was seven the cathedral library was getting rid of mahogany cases, and so half my room was taken over by a vitrine—my first—in which I would arrange and rearrange my objects, turn the key and open up the case on request. It was my *Wunderkammer*, my world of things, my secret history of touch" (351). Having made various historical and intimate connections to the world of things, his own secret history of touch, de Waal concludes by placing his latest vitrine "next to the piano, unlocked, so that the children can open the door if they wish" (351). Having displayed the netsukes, he marvels at their disarray, the evidence of ongoing circulation, touch, and caress. Slipping one of these precious objects into his own pocket, he heads back to his study to make more pots.

I have a medical cabinet in my dining room, a gift from my mother, purchased from an antique dealer in Delaware. This cabinet functions like de Waal's childhood vitrine. It is my own *"Wunderkammer*, my world of things, my secret history of touch."* In my vitrine there are still pots my potter gave me. They stand alongside other precious objects: a beautiful crystal vase, a gift from a family friend to celebrate my completing my doctoral degree; gifts from my students—a small, elegant handmade wooden bowl brought back from Central America; thrift store finds, among them a prewar Czechoslovakian porcelain juice set, the pitcher a vivid cobalt blue; my silver baby cup; a paper flower made by my Swiss godchild, the daughter of my first doctoral student. And recently I placed a sterling-silver Kiddush set that had belonged to my maternal grandmother on the bottom shelf of this cabinet. I am not sure how I will keep the silver polished, but I like having it here. There are now fewer pots than there used to be; initially, there were only pots. Some of them now reside in my kitchen cabinets; a few have broken. But those that remain share this sacred space with other precious objects that continue to move in and out of my life. This cabinet holds so many memories of my life before and after the rape. As I turn the old handle to open the unlocked door, I am reminded of that shattering. I can touch and engage with these treasured objects, material memories of my past. Yet I can gently close the door, leaving them safe.

The objects in De Waal's extraordinary family memoir bind his narrative to other, more quotidian collections that form the archeology of personal and communal histories of trauma. Strangely similar to the more ordinary natural history of de Waal's boyhood collecting, the "bones, a mouse skin, shells, a tiger's claw," and even "Victorian pennies" (350) evoke the history that took them all away, the rise of Nazism and the confiscation of virtually everything that had belonged to this family of collectors, along with the possession of so many European Jews, the poor as well as the rich.

The Allure of Pottery in My Afterlife

As a potter, I find it a bit strange when people who have my pots talk of them as if they are alive. I am not sure if I can cope with the afterlife of what I have made. But some objects do seem to retain the pulse of their making. (16)

Objects have always been carried, sold, bartered, stolen, retrieved and lost. People have always given gifts. It is how you tell their stories that matters. (348)

There is a vessel, one of many that my potter gave me not long after I was raped. At least this is how I remember it. It is a salt-fired piece, not porcelain like those made by Edmund de Waal.[11] It is rough and distorted, a singular object. It came into my home, the scene of the crime, later, well after that night's events. Maggie Nelson might say that it was "an import to the scene," but its belated arrival makes that technical designation impossible.

This piece began its existence on a potter's wheel, only later to be reshaped by hand. The potter tested its limits, distending, stressing, and reconstituting its contours with his hands. It stands only about six inches tall. As I go to take this measurement, pulling the piece out of its resting place in the repurposed medical cabinet that houses it, I notice other things. I am struck by the date carved into its base, 4/89. I am confused. I had thought that this piece was made in response to my rape. And yet it was made months earlier. Perhaps it was shaped in April but fired the following winter?

Taking in this date, I begin to see other things that contradict my memory of this gift. I had always imagined this pot as battered and strangely wounded, with a singular bandage-like patch near its lip. What I see instead are two patches. The vessel is more symmetrical than I remembered. The wound that had so moved me is not one but two bandage-like patches, one on either side. I now wonder if they are the remains of what might have been thwarted handles. Pressed too close to the surface of the pot, it seems that they were unable to serve that function. Unlike an actual bandage that clings to the surface of the skin, made to blend in not only through its color (that awful "flesh" color that is all about a kind of whiteness, or more recent transparent versions) but through its thinness, designed to cover the wound snugly and smoothly, the patches on the pot are three-dimensional. They are much more intrusive than a bandage, exaggerated by the very fact of their being made out of clay. I keep wanting to write about these clay bandages in the singular, but there is not just one wound.

Despite blending into the pockmarked green shades of the pot's salt-fired surface, these patches stand out. The rough, lichen-like texture of the glaze suggests something organic, as opposed to handmade. The pot appears to be ancient, found, earthen. This is part of what attracts me to its glaze, its patina. This is decidedly not a porcelain vessel.

I am finding this difficult to write. I want to get it right, but I have mixed feelings about my misremembering, about the potter, about that time, and about my relationship with clay. I was startled to find myself in Mexico in the winter of 2016 reading Edmund de Waal's *The White Road: Journey into an Obsession*, about porcelain, and thinking about my own fascination with and love of pottery. I realized that I had not considered how any of my desires bound me to my potter and all the gifts he gave me—both bowls that I use every day and decorative pieces prominently displayed in my home. All of this pottery has been with me for some thirty years, populating my life after my rape, constituting the interior spaces I have since called home.

As I first wrote down some of these thoughts, I checked to see if this potter had ever read the note I sent him on Facebook acknowledging this connection. I wrote from Mexico to say that I was reading about porcelain and writing about de Waal and was thinking of him. I told him that I hoped he was still making pots. Though we have not been friends for a very long time, the process of writing about Edmund de Waal has forced me to consider again these connections, the love and care my potter extended to me then and the pots that are still with me now. There is a tenderness that permeates these pieces. That potter had been there for me, at least for a time. I was held, and that memory is made material in these vessels. They are evidence of that time and that place. They are its remains.

Precarium: Holocaust Objects

What does it mean to engage with material objects and the materiality of texts that emerged from the Holocaust, texts that are similar to those that were once in the possession of de Waal's great-grandfather? That carefully curated library of rare books and manuscripts was never returned. It is now the property of the Austrian state and its national collection.

I am reminded of Bożena Shallcross's lush reading of more ordinary Holocaust texts in her study *The Holocaust Object in Polish and Polish-Jewish Culture*. Shallcross "take[s] pains to describe these texts . . . as both material thing[s] and written document[s]," and she applies the term "precarium" to these objects. With great precision, she explains that this term, "in its original legal context describes the deposit of items slated to be returned to their owners upon a positive change of situation." It also implies the shaky, unstable, precarious status of Holocaust texts and objects of various kinds. Despite presumably being held, she explains, "they wander and their very existence is threatened as they changed hands and places in diverse chance-driven scenarios."[12]

And yet for those of us writing now, those of us who have no family collections, the assembled material objects increasingly jog our memory: piles of shoes, stacks of suitcases, a tangle of eyeglasses, bales of human hair.[13] Their physical presence commands our attention. We find ourselves back at the legal definition of precarium as we take on the task of returning the provenance of these objects to their rightful owners by telling what stories we can, partial and incomplete tales that draw on the intimacy of the proximity between the object—a netsuke, a pair of shoes, a suitcase, a single pair of eyeglasses, a lock of hair, a pair of sweatpants—and those to whom these objects once belonged.[14]

If we consider the return of property as a form of doing justice, we must focus intently on how this tale of rescue lands a collection back in the hands of a family. The tale of precarious and unexpected return told in part 3 of *The Hare with Amber Eyes*, "Vienna, Kövecses, Tunbridge Wells, Vienna 1938–1947," challenges both the legal meaning of precarium and the broader desire to find justice in the restitution of stolen property. As the netsukes changed hands and places, their existence was threatened. And yet the chance-driven scenario at the heart of this story leaves us surprised by the possibility of return and recognition well outside of the bounds of the law.

"The Tears of Things"

Viktor, the head of the Ephrussi family, was virtually destitute in the final years of his life. Living with his daughter and her family in a modest home in a London suburb, he still held on to the key to his precious, once carefully locked library, like those Sephardic Jews who kept the keys to their families' lost homes. Edmund de Waal presents his father's memories of this man, recounting the classically educated grandfather's retelling the children an ancient tale. "Aeneas and his return from Carthage. There, on the walls, are scenes of Troy. It is only then, confronted by the image of what he has lost, that Aeneas finally weeps. *Sunt lacrimae rerum.* Aeneas says. These are the tears of things, he reads, at the kitchen table as the boys try to finish their algebra" (270).[15] We touch this grandfather's grief in the tears of things. Viktor died in that London suburb and was buried there, not far from that kitchen table, worlds away from the majestic monuments where the rest of his family were laid to rest.

As the Gestapo carefully attended to sorting, annotating, and packaging up the family's holdings, Anna, the family's maid, saved the netsuke collection bit by bit. She placed a few netsukes in her pocket each day. While silver—a whole room worth of cutlery and serving pieces large and small—a gold service, all of the jewelry, a library of books, and a grand collection of artworks, furniture, and exquisite china (whole sets of dishes along with all kinds of larger, more obviously decorative objects) were taken away, Anna quietly culled a few netsukes at a time from that black-lacquered vitrine, took them to her room, and hid them in her mattress for the duration of the war.

De Waal writes, "The survival of the netsuke in Anna's pocket, in her mattress, is an affront. I cannot bear for it to slip into symbolism. Why should they have got through this war in a hiding-place, when so many hidden people did not? I can't make people and places and things fit together any more. These stories unravel me" (283). The pieces do not all come together, and yet in this chance-driven scenario, the netsukes are returned. Anna hands them over to Elisabeth, the author's grandmother.

Dispersion and the Possible: Life After

My relationship with my potter concluded long ago. Not only did that relationship end; the intellectual life I began as a religious studies major at Brown also ended. I did not become a theologian, but I am a scholar of religion. Disappointed by both God and the law, I have had to find other ways of living on.

I put my faith in the poet's and the potter's hands. Writing, like making new pots out of old clay, helps contain brokenness and can even make it beautiful. Over these many years, I have crafted many words to contain my pain, none of which are definitive. We keep writing, trying to breathe new life into traumatic pasts, pointing toward different futures. We also have other containers for the brokenness, gifts—Maggie Nelson's glass box, Edmund de Waal's netsukes, my pots—to remind us of the passage of time. We can be surprised by what comes after we put these gifts to different uses—a repurposed medical cabinet, a decommissioned vitrine, the collections they hold.

Objects make the past tangible, but they cannot erase the break. There is no going back to what had been. But we need to keep telling stories. Objects hold out the promise of finding something of ourselves. And, if we are lucky, we may find our voices in the narratives of others, making all of us less lonely and the world, perhaps, more beautiful.

PART 2

The Arts and Rites of Holding

CHAPTER 4

The Art of Custody
Police Property Management

Searching for Evidence

During the summer of 2008 I went to Harvard University to begin work on this book. I started by asking questions about custody. I wanted to understand the laws that surround criminal holdings. Mostly, I wanted to understand how it was possible that, more than thirty years later, Jane Mixer's clothing could find its way to court. How did that work? I got a small research grant from my university and headed to Harvard's law library, only to learn on my first day there that my questions were "extralegal." What the law offers are rules of evidence and the crucial "chain of custody," but the holding of criminal evidence, especially in violent criminal cases, is the work of local police and some courts. The rules and procedures that govern evidence are diffuse. As with election procedures, each district or precinct has its own policies and practices. But it was in those august halls of legal learning that I stumbled on the only publications about these practices. And these works in turn led me to people engaged in trying to professionalize those practices.

Later that summer, following up on references I'd gathered, I called Joseph Latta, founder and president of the International Association for Property and Evidence (IAPE). He explained that there were only two books on the subject of property management and that he had written or co-written both of them. He also told me more about the IAPE and allowed me to join. I have been an associate member ever since, receiving

Fig. 4. Mike Mandel and Larry Sultan, *Untitled*.
From *Evidence*, 1977. © Mike Mandel, © Larry
Sultan / Courtesy of Mike Mandel and Estate of
Larry Sultan.

regular copies of the IAPE's publication *The Evidence Log*. Not only
that, but in the spring of 2009 I was able to take a two-day IAPE training, one of the professional development courses the organization runs
throughout the United States. Usually called "Property and Evidence
Management in Law Enforcement," these classes are hands-on work-
shops that train police professionals whose job it is to handle evidence
and store property in locations large and small.

The IAPE Course

On March 19 and 20, 2009, I participated in this IAPE class alongside forty law enforcement officials. This IAPE seminar, sponsored by the Lower Merion Township Police Department, was held at the Montgomery County Public Safety Training Campus located in Conshohocken, Pennsylvania, not far from my home in Philadelphia. Like me, most of the other participants came from the Philadelphia area, though a few hailed from more distant locales: Fort Meade, Maryland, Rehoboth Beach, Delaware, South Orange, New Jersey, New York City, and in two cases all the way from Hastings, Minnesota.

The class met from 8:00 to 5:00 on the first day and from 8:00 to 4:30 on the second, with an hour for lunch, although the first day there was a lunch presentation from a company that sells barcoding equipment. That lunch was optional, but I attended. The company provided pizza and much food for thought. Their pitch was library science meets criminal justice—and they sold catalogues and retrieval systems that shelve and warehouse guns, bloody garments, and drugs. The barcoding equipment makes the retrieval of documents and materials much more efficient. For larger precincts and storage facilities, such technology can be crucial. It may also not be an option, given the cost.

My classmates included detectives and special agents, a police chief, sergeants and lieutenants, patrol officers, and investigators. There was also an "evidence custodian" and an "evidence lab technician," and two probation officers. There were only a handful of women, though the group as a whole was racially and ethnically diverse. I was the only person present who was not a criminal justice professional.

We were provided with large spiral notebooks containing course materials. As the text explained, the goal of the course was "to provide a frame work of legal and ethical requirements in the operation of law enforcement property and evidence units; to acquaint individuals with the technicalities and responsibilities involved in the daily function of a property unit; to provide a positive learning environment for property and evidence professionals to exchange ideas and concepts." The class was built around an elaborate set of PowerPoint slides that were reproduced in miniature in the pages of the notebook along with room for individual notes. My notebook is peppered with my annotations, and rereading those notes years later, I am keenly aware of my own preoccupations. But I am getting ahead of myself. I want to offer a brief overview of the topics covered and the logic of the class. After introductions, the first unit addressed headlines and liabilities, the problems that can plague those doing this work and often the only occasions for public engagement. When something goes wrong, the property room can be a huge liability. These topics framed the work of the course. From these cautionary tales, we turned to policies, procedures, and packaging, then to documentation, numbering, the movement of set property, and the documentation of those practices.

The afternoon sessions that first day covered the most challenging cases of documentation: firearms, narcotics, and currency. These three types of evidence are the most contentious, and handling them correctly is absolutely vital to the integrity of the property room. The class then turned to recent events and trends. These topics included the AIDS virus, the terrorist attacks of September 11, 2001, home foreclosures, the price of oil ($150 a barrel at the time), and DNA-evidence retention, among other things.

Of special interest to me were the issue of securing evidence in homicides, sexual assaults, and capital crimes and the challenges of long-term retention of that evidence.[1] In relation to DNA, there were questions about postconviction appeals, the statute of limitation, the Innocence Project and state innocence commissions, John Doe warrants, and state-operated evidence warehouses. Taking its cue from the news of the day, this up-to-the-minute course addressed a series of actual cases and some of the challenges they pose for property custodians. As we shall see, these issues remain abiding concerns in cases where rules differ from state to state.

After addressing current trends, the class went on to consider management concerns. These range from issues of staffing and the chain of command, to time management and training, to technical details involving the receipt, storage, purging, and removal of evidence. I learned that purging is vital because storage facilities are often filled to excess. The final two units on that first day simply delved more deeply into these matters, focusing first on training and then on the purging and disposition of evidence.

The second day began where the first left off. The matter of the disposition of evidence includes the diversion of property, "the process by which the ownership of abandoned, forfeited, or unclaimed property is legally transferred to a public agency for public use,"[2] the documentation of these procedures at each point in the process, and finally, in some cases, actions taken to get rid of the excess when these materials are no longer legally salient.

We then turned to audits and inventories, security, and even the layout of the property room. The afternoon session covered issues of temporary storage, including the short-term storage of biohazards and shelving and storage techniques, with special attention to guns, money, and drugs, the most dangerous and challenging items held in these facilities. This part of the seminar was specifically addressed to the professionals in charge and the kinds of challenges posed by these forms of evidence. We heard cautionary tales about former participants in the course who found themselves in legal trouble because they handled evidence improperly; some of them even ended up in jail.

The course ended with instruction on constructing storage facilities and how to move collections of evidence. In retrospect, I am struck by the importance of this aspect of evidence management, because I now know that since 1989, the Atlanta police have moved evidence to three different storage facilities. My evidence may have been lost in any one of these moves, if not in the original storage facility.

DNA: Current Trends (2009)

Revisiting my notes from the IAPE course, I found extensive annotations about DNA and changing laws that govern how long states keep evidence in cases of sexual assault and homicide, including capital cases. With the advent of DNA testing, these rules continue to evolve. The slides we saw offered the following examples, though—alas—there was no reference to the laws in Georgia:

Illinois, 2002, keep homicide evidence forever
New York, 2006, keep sexual assault evidence forever
Massachusetts, 2006, keep sexual assault evidence for 27 years
Colorado, 2008, keep capital crime evidence, until defendant's death

From another slide, we learned that unsolved homicide cases in Pennsylvania are left open for seventy-five years—or for less time if all involved in the case have died. What was new in 2009 was a federal law associated with the Violence Against Women Act that gathered rape kit evidence even from women who did not want to be identified. The law referred to these as Jane Doe rape kits. The slide read that as of January 1, 2009, keeping these kits would become the law of the land: "Any state that gets federal funds/grants from the Violence Against Women Act, is required to have implemented by January 2009 a plan for women to [be] examined for a sexual assault and not have to [have] reported being assaulted. The hospital, etc. who administers the sexual assault exam must keep the rape kit without any identification other than a distinct number. The victim can decide, within a designated period of time, to report the assault to the police." The text of the slide then assessed the challenges of implementing this new law. "Here is where it gets crazy. . . . There are no guidelines as to who, where or how to store the sexual assault kits. Some states say it stays at the hospital. Some say it goes to the District Attorney; yet other states say that the kits are turned over to the police who will retain them."

The final line on the slide read, "Impact upon property rooms??? We will probably get it." This 2009 regulation reveals the ongoing challenges surrounding even rape kits that have been identified and how they do or do not get processed. The backlog of rape kits was then, and remains, staggering. And all of this falls in the laps of those who run often underfunded property rooms. We learned in 2009 that processing an individual rape kit could cost $500; as the massive backlogs were becoming known, even matching grants from private foundations had barely scratched the surface. In other words, there was a huge number of unprocessed rape kits in storage facilities across the country, and this is still the case in 2020, more than a decade later.[3] I also learned from the IAPE materials that DNA evidence is vital not only in cases of murder and violent sexual assault but in solving burglary and other forms of theft as well. The challenge is how to get all of this DNA evidence into the FBI's "Combined DNA Index System" (CODIS).[4]

Having learned about all this from the IAPE, I was more than prepared to learn that my rape kit had probably never been processed and could not be located. Mine is just one of the millions of cases in evidentiary limbo. The Jane Doe law, although well-meaning, revealed that there was already a serious problem with the processing and storage of rape kits, even those that were clearly identified with the names of women who, like me, were more than willing to report these crimes.

Not only is there an enormous backlog of untested rape kits, but the kits themselves warrant further scrutiny as objects. In her study *Anthem*, artist and scholar Aliza Shvarts conducted a comparative analysis of the different sexual assault evidence collection kits used in the United States (see figs. 5a and 5b). Produced by both commercial companies and state agencies, kits usually take the form of a box or envelope that contains medical and forensic tools of capture (envelopes, swabs, bags, etc.). As Shvarts discovered, they vary widely: a kit might contain seven

Fig. 5. Aliza Shvarts, *Anthem*, 2019, (a) installation view and (b) close-up view. *In Practice: Other Objects*, SculptureCenter, New York, 2019. Courtesy of the artist. Photos: Kyle Knodell.

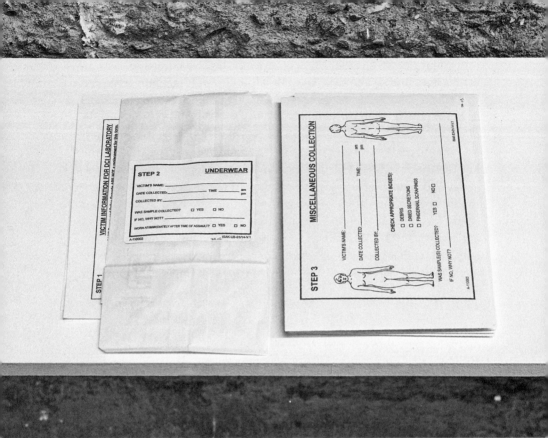

Fig. 5b.

or twenty-one steps; it might use legal or medical language ("victim" vs. "patient") and gendered or gender-neutral terms ("panties" vs. "underwear").[5]

In order to appreciate the relationship between this systemic problem and the rituals and rites of custody, let us look at how those who work to professionalize custodial and evidentiary practices write about the nature of their work. We will then examine the connection between the law and its attention to the "chain of custody" and the tense intersection of these practices.

Labors of Custody

The term "custody" derives from the Middle English verb *to guard*, the noun form being *guardianship*. In the case of children, the word tends to trigger memories of courtroom battles.[6] But custody applies not only to children but also to prisoners, those cared for, supervised, or controlled as determined by a court of law. The term applies as well to both persons and property. More specifically, according to the *American Heritage Dictionary*, custody refers to the state of "being detained or held under guard by the police," or it may simply refer to the care, supervision, and control exerted by one in charge, a concept that emerges in the legal sphere but has broader implications. Here, the domestic and the legal/criminal are intimately bound. Courts can and often do connect the two senses of the term. Children need protection and must be attended to. In custody, they are cared for, guarded, supervised, and otherwise kept presumably, ideally, out of harm's way. Prisoners (or alleged criminals) obviously need the same kind of care and supervision, but they, unlike children, have done harm; they need to be in custody, but their custodians also need protection.

When custody is applied to property rather than to people, the term refers to material objects held by police or courts. These objects, evidence in criminal cases, must be guarded—ironically—so as to be kept pristine. If evidentiary property is tampered with or otherwise disturbed, its viability as legal evidence is compromised. When we think about custody of children or the elderly, or even of criminals, custody is very much an active thing. It requires daily support and sustenance. In the case of objects, by contrast, custody requires something more like benign neglect.

According to the law, the active part of the custodial process is not custody itself but rather its acquisition. The provenance of evidence in a criminal case is "the chain of custody," a series of moves that constitute the acquisition and proper housing of evidence. Acquisition is only the prelude to custody. In this linear narrative, acquisition and processing lead to a final resting place: custody. It is as if once the evidence is in a secure storage room, superintendence, trust, or guardianship has been secured once and for all time. The labor of this form of holding or keeping becomes invisible. With no need for food or exercise, objects find their place on shelves, in boxes, and in bags, and they stay there, in some cases, seemingly in perpetuity. And yet, as we have seen, keeping track of such objects, and making sure that they are properly labeled, processed, and stored, requires attention and ongoing engagement.[7]

As I consider the process that creates custody, I am reminded of its fragility, and of all the things that can go wrong in the daily labor of guardianship and custodial care. To apprehend what is taken for granted about the practices of custody, we need to notice them, pay attention to them, and determine how they operate. In other words, we need to know why the practices of custody have been so underappreciated and undervalued (and, usually, underfunded); and we need to find the points of entry, the threads we can take hold of to begin to unravel these mechanisms. Seeing how these practices align with what it means to care for people rather than to warehouse material property is one such thread.

I now want to examine how the professionalization of these practices, the kind of work that the IAPE does, disrupts their invisibility. Efforts to make the system work better, like those of the IAPE, challenge a fundamental tenet of the law: its static notion of custody, in which custody is seen only as a noun, as the end point of the labor that goes into amassing evidence. Students in IAPE and similar courses operate under a kind of supplementary logic that is both additive and potentially transformative of the law. The more professionalized this labor becomes, and the more we notice instances of mismanagement, and the more we see the problems with the status quo, the more urgent and radical such an intervention becomes.

The Chain of Custody

The IAPE has not only codified best practices overall; it has also attempted to rethink the chain of custody so as to cover the work of property management, or custody. Using the chain of custody, the IAPE promotes a more expansive notion of this legal concept. According to the glossary of key terms on the IAPE's website, "chain of custody refers to the chronological documentation of the seizure, custody, control, transfer (temporary or permanent), and disposition of evidence, either physical or electronic."

This description is an advance over earlier efforts to define this critical legal term, one in which documentation is crucial. The seizure, custody, control, transfer, and disposition of criminal evidence must be recorded in writing. In his earlier book *Property and Evidence by the Book: Everything You Ever Wanted to Know About the Management of a Property and Evidence Room* (2004), IAPE president Joseph Latta quotes criminologist George Rush in saying that the chain of custody is a "formal written process recording the persons having custody of evidence from initial point of receipt or custody to final disposition. The record also reflects the dates and reasons evidence is transferred from one location or person to another."[8]

The latter definition interests me more deeply, because it is more directly linked to the legal category and because it is more expansive, covering not only the acquisition of evidence but the ongoing work of custody, the holding and processing of objects over time, from start to finish. The chain of custody serves as a legal container for this ongoing labor, with links continually added to the narrative of these objects.[9] It encompasses who has them at any given moment, where that person has taken them, how and by whom they have been processed, and whether and when they are appropriately disposed of or put to other use. I like the idea of the links in the chain, each piece of the process narrated. Although this is still a teleological account of the chain of custody, it has more room. Custody is not merely an end point but a longer set of processes and procedures covered by the law. I like the idea that both the dates of and the reasons for moving or transferring property are part of the story. I also like knowing the names and provenance of all the people who have come into contact with these objects; all are part of the story.[10] Someone actually carries them from one place to the next, enacting care and guardianship.

The IAPE describes the narrative account of the chain of custody as a "formal written process recording." Outside law enforcement, there is a large body of literature on this kind of writing. According to the Fordham School of Social Work, "process recordings" are crucial to social work. As the school explains on its website—and most schools of social work have similar materials—these reports are at the heart of social work education. In introducing its "process recording handbook," the

Fordham program emphasizes that "in writing process recordings, the students are asked to listen and observe carefully, to recall and review their work, and to examine the feelings it engenders in them. It is a tool with which to record their thoughts, feelings, and analysis of the work as it unfolds."[11] This does not match exactly George Rush's description of the chain of custody, but it does resonate with the kind of tender care I describe as the labor of custody. Listening and observing carefully, recording and reviewing one's work, are in fact what the property custodian must do to complete and respect the integrity of the chain of custody. The attention to detail required of the social work student as an act of care and respect resonates with the connecting links in the chain of custody. Although neither Latta nor Rush emphasizes the plotting of various "thoughts, feelings, and analysis," the chain of custody is a kind of case file, with the property officer or manager[12] in the role of the social worker.

Like a social worker, with her responsibility to her client, the property room professional is also a caretaker. "Regardless [of] what they are called," Latta and Rush explain, "they are one of the most important segments within the agency [law enforcement]. Simply stated, without a well-managed evidence and property unit the prosecuting attorney would not be able to file charges, let alone obtain convictions. The diligent work of investigators and all others involved in a case can go up in a puff of smoke."[13] For Latta and Rush, this comes down to the question of trust. Can we trust these officials and their work—delivering, seizing, recording, and safeguarding evidence? Do these professionals adhere to the highest standards of ethics in their work? Without this basic trust, the whole legal system is unable to function.

Laws of Evidence

Having looked more closely at what the police professionals have to say about the work of custody, I returned to the files I compiled in Cambridge to see how the legal literature on "evidence" matched up. I consulted several texts, among them *The Federal Rules of Evidence*; *Getting Your Hands on the Evidence*; *The Elements of Evidence*; *Model Code of Evidence*; *Evidence in Trials at Common Law*; *Federal Rules of Evidence Digest*; and the *Introduction to Criminal Evidence and Court*

Procedures.[14] These legal texts spell out the rules and regulations regarding criminal evidence; they address everything from how photographs can and cannot be used in court to the handling and viability of material objects in custody and the courtroom. In these sources, the ongoing labor of treating such objects seems at best to be folded into the "chain of custody." In many of these texts, the crucial questions concern the admissibility of evidence. Increasingly, scientific evidence has to do with both the provenance of material objects and quantification. In a sense, these concerns parallel the labor involved in custody more broadly construed. No evidence ever "speaks for itself." In all cases, material evidence must be verified by the testimony of reliable witnesses who attest that these objects are indeed what the prosecuting or defense attorneys say they are. Here again, it is human labor that gives voice, power, and legal weight to objects, enabling these silent witnesses to speak. The people who take care of evidence and move it safely and incorruptibly from storage to the courtroom, and those who verify the objects' authenticity on the stand, constitute critical invisible extralegal labor. Both are crucial to making the procedures of evidence work. They enable the objects to speak and the law to function.[15]

Containing Loss: Circling the Crime Scene

I began writing this chapter years ago. It was the first writing I did toward what would become this book. But as I returned to those early pages, I did not recognize what I now understand this chapter is about. In that nascent writing, I could not allow myself to get too close. I found myself at the outermost perimeters of the material, as if circling a crime scene from as far away as possible. Many years later, trying to edit, organize, and tell this story, I became keenly aware of that distance.

For a long time, when asked, "What is your book all about?," I would retreat from the heart of my story and talk about this chapter, about the police and the property room. This was a comfort only because I hadn't yet allowed myself to admit that this chapter has always been about my attempt to reckon with what I had once thought justice might be for me. And so, returning to that earlier writing, I realized how far I had been from this central concern. I had begun at the outermost edges of this story. This was easy and safe, the stuff of police procedurals, highlighting evidence but hiding the labor that goes into it. I did not have to talk about the contamination, corruption, and loss of evidence at the heart of this book.

In that early writing, I asked, "Why are collections of criminal evidence so hard to talk about, and why is grasping the work of custody, the labor involved in holding these pieces of evidence, so difficult?" I had assumed that this was a legal question, but I learned that I was mistaken. Because it fell outside the framework of the law, I had to consider the status of both the evidence held and those whose job it was to maintain large and widely dispersed criminal collections. I learned about police procedures and their precarious and necessary relationship to the law. But what helped me grasp the paradox of custody—how it is both central and invisible at once—came from another realm entirely. Feminist historian Joan Scott has characterized this dynamic as the logic of the supplement. According to Scott, this logic marks the irony of the centrality and yet extraneous status of women in history. The necessity and yet the superfluity of women's role in history is similar to the strange status of custody in the work of the law. Despite being critical to the law, custody—the holding of evidence—remains an afterthought. I realized that in those initial pages, written decades ago, I had given a careful and thorough reading of Scott's essay "Women's History" but had never returned to my story. I did this close reading just to be sure that I had gotten it right. But in all those pages, I never got to the question of justice. I hadn't yet understood how holding on to criminal evidence, to all those fragile objects, might serve auspicious ends.

My own less than conscious move to the periphery was itself a kind of holding back. My distant and abstract engagement was my own version of containment, a form of self-protection. I was keeping some of the most painful pieces of this project at a distance, only beginning to address them from afar. This chapter documents my move from the outskirts to close proximity to my case. It shows how I came to take custody of my own story, including the evidence in my rape case—my rape kit, my linens, my sweatpants—what was and what was not taken into custody. Even now, with the crime report in my hands, I know very little. Yet I needed to try to imagine what had happened to my belongings, where they might be. I needed to get behind the scenes to learn about their custody in order to reconstruct some semblance of their story and what that said about my own.

The container that I initially constructed still very much frames this chapter and how I think about these matters. But before getting further into that discussion, I need to acknowledge how these less than conscious efforts performed a different kind of labor. They kept at bay some of the most painful aspects of this work, my deep ambivalence around returning to my own literal crime scene and what, if anything, remained. Not knowing what (if any) physical evidence was left of my cold case kept all of this in motion for a long time (1989–2014). Something could still perhaps happen. Or not. The trail might still be live. If I had been raped in Massachusetts, the evidence would already have been purged. And although I had for a long time imagined titling the final chapter of this book "Nothing Left," this too was a fantasy, part of the allure of the finality of not knowing.

When I finally did contact the Atlanta police in 2014, I learned that they could not find any trace of the evidence from my case, now twenty-five years old. What did emerge was that the crime report included my victim statement, with handwritten edits, and my victim mug shot, taken that night, but not the inventory of physical evidence. I had prepared myself for the worst-case scenario, the possibility that nothing remained. As I have already indicated, I was shocked that there was anything left at all. But again I am getting ahead of myself.

Preparing for the worst so that whatever happens is only "half-bad at best"—this was my stance. This phrase came back to me from the distant past. It is uttered by Fairy May, a vulnerable woman confined to a sanitarium in John Patrick's 1950 play *The Curious Savage*, a character I played in a high school theater production. I have always found the words comforting, even protective, even as I am now acutely aware of what this position guards against. Thinking the worst and imagining it as only half-bad means not allowing oneself to feel what bad situations in fact make us feel. We close off the possibility. We refuse the vulnerability that we might actually experience. This is the logic I had deployed for so long in my case: if I always expected the worst, then whatever happened would be half-bad at best.

Out there on the perimeter of my cold crime scene, I was able to ask myself why criminal holdings are so invisible that the work of holding them is taken for granted, if not dismissed. I needed to think about what it meant to discover, in my first venture into this project, that custody was not exclusively a legal matter, that my questions were extralegal, even as I always already understood that without evidence there would be no criminal case. This was the puzzle that I began with, the contradiction that I needed to solve in order to work my way back to the scene. This was the logic of the supplement. It enabled me to get closer.

And so, by focusing on the arts of holding, I want to expose this essential but often supplemental piece of the criminal justice system. I pull back the curtain in order to shed new light on the arts of holding, so as to remember and give validity to my evidence and help others appreciate the importance of this unacknowledged labor. My hope is that we might begin to tell more stories about criminal cases, like my own, that may never make it to court, narratives not unlike those told by Edmund de Waal and Maggie Nelson.

A Supplement to History

In many ways, but perhaps most especially in police property rooms, the object as evidence, as legal exhibit, may be the most obvious case of the relationships among holding, memory, and the work of justice. We hold evidence in custody with the promise that it will eventually make its way to court, so that justice, if only juridical justice, can be done. This is a familiar story, rare in practice but potent nonetheless. We hold on to evidence. And yet we rarely consider the ongoing labor involved in that holding. Instead, we often take for granted that evidence is safe and easily accessible, available when and if it is ever needed, as it was in Jane Mixer's case.

The relationship between evidentiary objects and those who attend to them in storage facilities has been at the heart of this chapter. Because custodial work happens behind the scenes, we hardly notice that it is happening or see those who do it. Storage facilities and their holdings depend upon the cyclical daily tasks of custodial labor. And, for the most part, those engaged in these tasks in the criminal justice system learn them on the job, with little if any professional training. The invisibility of their labor is in keeping with the dismissed nature of custodial work—the domestic, feminized, low-level tasks of cleaning and organizing, the routines of maintenance workers, caretakers, cleaning people, and domestic help.

The law focuses on the "chain of custody," or the provenance of evidence. It is not concerned with what happens between the time when it is seized and whether and when it is ever summoned. Custody, though, is a practice critical to maintaining the integrity of physical evidence, and to our ongoing ability to retrieve such objects when they are, in effect, called to testify. As we have seen, the labor of custody—of care—the undervalued work at the heart of any criminal case, echoes Joan Scott's account of the logic of the supplement. But the resonances are deeper.

In *A Room of One's Own*, Virginia Woolf asks, "Why . . . not add a supplement to history? calling it, of course, by some inconspicuous name so that women might figure there with impropriety?" In showing the ruse of this innocuous move, revealing the irony in Woolf's appeal for a mere supplement, Scott explains, "The delicate sarcasm of her comments about an 'inconspicuous name' and the need for propriety suggest a complicated project (she calls it 'ambitious beyond my daring') that, even as she tries to circumscribe the difficulties, evokes contradictory implications. Women are both added to history and they occasion its rewriting, they provide something extra and they are necessary for completion, they are superfluous and indispensable."[16]

This intervention, the adding of women to history that Woolf describes, is both inconsequential and necessary. This tension is what attracts me to Scott's logic of the supplement in trying to get at the work of custody. And it resonates in fascinating ways with how police property management, like so much domestic labor, is gratuitous and yet invaluable. For both Jacques Derrida and Virginia Woolf, according to Joan Scott, the supplement "is something added, extra, superfluous, above and beyond what is already fully present; it is also a replacement for what is absent, missing, lacking, thus required for completion or wholeness. 'The supplement is neither a plus nor a minus, neither an outside nor the complement of an inside, neither accident nor essence.' It is (in Barbara Johnson's words) 'superfluous and necessary, dangerous and redemptive.'"[17] The work of the supplement is how I think about the logic of custody, a domestic term and set of tasks that is both additive and necessary, a minor part of, and yet essential to, the operation of the law.

For Scott, "the seemingly modest request that history be supplemented with information about women suggests not only that history as it is, is incomplete, but also that historians' mastery of the past is necessarily partial."[18] My own claim is that the whole subject of custody has been rendered invisible in the realm of adjudication despite its centrality. This allegedly minor addition to our legal thinking—attention to the labor of custody—turns out to be vital to the law and its operation. It is both absolutely necessary and heretofore taken for granted.

Holdings

A criminal case in some ways arrests the past, holding it in custody, but the past is not static, even when there is a verdict. Part of what attracts me to the notion of holding is the way in which holding signals the relationship between memories and object. Because they are held, these objects can be carried forward, helping us tell new stories.

Holding signals the relationship between objects and memory. Memories like us to pay attention to the details. Holding on too tightly or not carefully enough, such memories, like delicate objects, can break, and of course painful memories are often tied up in the objects that both hold and carry these legacies forward. These are the very qualities that mark how both the poet and the potter have helped me give voice to my story. We do justice to different violent pasts through Holocaust objects, precaria, and individual pieces of criminal evidence like my sweatpants or Jane Mixer's wool jumper.[19]

Let me say this differently. Touching the past is implicit in the act of holding. As we have already seen, even metaphorically we tap into a discourse of the tangible. We hold objects, shards of our violent pasts, in our hands, and if we are attentive, careful, we can keep what they signal alive. Like the barrister in the film *Denial* who picks up a piece of mangled wire in the ruins of the crematoria at Auschwitz-Birkenau, and keeps it with him as he defends Deborah Lipstadt in the British High Court of Justice, such objects can prevent us from forgetting. Although it is a fictional enactment, gesturing with this talisman demonstrates how objects often work to animate and compel memory. The film taps into this all too familiar act. Memory objects can function as prompts, as physical reminders that keep memory alive and vivid.

The Logic of the Supplement in the Evidence Room
In the first chapter of Joseph Latta and George Rush's book on management and organization, there is a brief introduction devoted to the "legal aspects" of this work:

> In terms of economics, the consequences of the mismanagement of property and evidence are staggering. But in terms of the judicial process, where the burden of proof often rests in the presentation of physical evidence, mismanagement is tantamount to legal malfeasance. As previously stated, mismanagement often results in charges not being filed or may result in an unsuccessful prosecution. Through the mass media (press and television) disclosures of irregularities can cause embarrassment to the agency and to the profession as a whole. This is compounded by a loss of public confidence. Departments can also face possible civil liabilities (lawsuits) and other claims against the agency. Supervisorial shortfalls falling under the category of "personnel problems" are generally the leading cause of mismanagement.[20]

Like the logic of the supplement, these efforts are both additive and essential, in Scott's formulation.

In Joseph Latta's updated manual, *Property and Evidence by the Book*, there is no reference to the legal aspects of this work. These important implications of property management are simply assumed, taken for granted. But in the book written with Rush, the criminologist, this opening paragraph frames both the first chapter and the book as a whole. It describes in broad strokes the crucial nature of this work. What is striking about this account is how matter-of-fact it is in making its case. Of course, the authors acknowledge the staggering economic implications of mismanagement; only then do they turn to the legal implications. This echoes Virginia Woolf's opening to *A Room of One's Own*, where Woolf suggests adding a supplement to history to account for women. When the subject of the law is broached in the second sentence of this brief paragraph, it begins with the word *but*. "But in terms of the judicial process, where the burden of proof often rests in the presentation of physical evidence, mismanagement is tantamount to legal malfeasance."

Because the burden of proof is apt to depend on the physical evidence held in police custody, mismanagement is intolerable, "tantamount to legal malfeasance," unacceptable to public officials, let alone to victims. And yet despite the importance of this labor to the workings of the law, those who do this work have little public standing, authority, or stature. Their misconduct is nevertheless a major problem for law enforcement. They can become the source of scandal and loss of public trust in the entire system. And so the paragraph, and indeed the entire section on legal implications, ends on this cautionary note: trust is crucial. If the persons responsible for evidence and the chain of custody are not trustworthy and competent, entire police departments can be held liable. Everything seems to come down to who gets hired. The worst problems result from "supervisorial shortfalls" or personnel problems. And yet the minor players in the criminal justice system carry the burden of making sure that all material evidence is properly attended to so that it can be presented in court. Such evidence can make or break a legal case.

According to the IAPE standards, the property official need not be a sworn officer. In fact, according to Latta and Rush, civilians are less likely than officers to get into legal trouble.[21] The primary tasks and duties of these officials are as follows:

- Preserve all incoming property from contamination
- Maintain and update property documentation with tracking information, commonly referred to as the "chain of custody"
- Ensure that all releases and dispositions of property are legal and properly documented
- Arrange and document interim releases and returns of property for court, crime lab analysis, or investigative use
- Operate computer terminals as needed
- Prepare and forward property-related forms to requesting units and agencies

- Serve as liaison between the agency and other local, state, and federal law enforcement agencies
- Maintain current knowledge of federal, state, and local laws related to property management
- Provide for maintenance of the storage facility
- Inventory property based on the policy demands of the agency. Ensure that all efforts are taken to make the property room as safe as possible for employees as well as property[22]

What is most striking here is that the "chain of custody" is but one item in the list of official responsibilities, yet each of these duties is tied to the legal questions of law enforcement and has broad ramifications for the chain of custody. Latta explains:

> The ultimate goal for any Property Officer is the appropriate disposition of property, whether in compliance with court order, through release to its rightful owner, or through other legal means such as auction, diversion, or destruction. Both management and supervision need to closely monitor the Property Officer's regular activities to ensure that priorities are established and properly implemented. Specific goals and objectives are needed to direct the Property Officer in completing certain tasks, such as regular purging. The property room needs the fulltime attention of a manager, both as a leader and as a monitor of policy and procedure.[23]

These standards, codified by the IAPE ("Standard #2, Staffing, Scheduling, etc., as of October 16, 2002"), appear straightforward enough. I call attention to them again to highlight the enormous responsibilities involved. Preserving the safety and integrity of evidence is not a minor task. It is absolutely essential to law enforcement. Without this labor, there is no credible evidence, and without evidence, there is no legal case. There is no criminal justice.

Custody, Containers, and Holding Memory

But we also keep vast storehouses of evidence, places that serve also as containers for memories associated with that evidence. As a plural noun, the term "holdings" refers to legally owned properties, usually capital or stock assets but also the materials that make up a library or archival collection. Pieces of criminal evidence once in custody are also considered legal holdings.

As an adjective, by contrast, "holding" can be an impediment. It tends to delay progress toward some desired end, as when we say that the work is "on hold." It can also refer to short-term storage or retention, as when an alleged criminal is kept in a holding cell, for example. And perhaps this adjective best expresses the hopeful teleological status of this kind of police facility. Like people kept in a holding tank or holding cell, objects kept in these places are imagined to be temporary residents. The promise of the legal definition of "precarium" comes to mind. Property is held until its rightful owner is found. And yet, in practice, this form of legal custody can be more permanent. Criminal justice facilities are increasingly set up for the long haul. In the case of violent crimes like murder and rape, such evidentiary holdings can be kept in perpetuity. These storage facilities are the kinds of places that Nelson describes, where all the numbered pieces of criminal evidence from her aunt's murder case were kept for all those years.

Criminal evidence is held in vast warehouses, institutions devoted to its organization and preservation. And not unlike these police property rooms, Holocaust archives, libraries, and museums are also committed to the preservation of evidentiary and often fragile holdings. In both kinds of institutional settings, objects are considered assets whose values are difficult to calculate. They are both priceless and oddly worthless, but they always demand tender care.

Evidence as Art / Holding the Past in Custody

Physical objects, though tangible, tend also to be fragile. To conserve rescued objects, as in the mission of the United States Holocaust Memorial Museum, means knowing how to hold on—how to maintain and keep those precious and vulnerable objects—how to attend to their special needs in order to keep them viable. I will turn to the case of the USHMM and its holdings in the next chapter, but the same practices are very much in keeping with the labors of police property management, the organizing and ongoing maintenance of criminal holdings held in evidence rooms across the United States. In both of these contexts, "touch" and even exposure to light can compromise attempts to rescue, preserve, and deploy such evidence.

In their 1977 collaboration *Evidence*, photographers Larry Sultan and Mike Mandel created "a book made up solely of pictures culled from vast industrial and governmental archives" (see figs. 4 and 6). As curator Carter Ratcliff explains, "For two and half years, they combed through the image-vaults of nearly eighty bureaucracies, federal agencies, aerospace corporations, university laboratories, fire and police departments."[24] The two young photographers opened up these archives "for the purposes of art while using them as a way to examine the society that produced them."[25] They took a different kind of custody of these preserved materials, granting them new life.

Sultan and Mandel examined what were often restricted legal, governmental, and industrial archives, especially in the aerospace industry. They tackled the archives of more than "one hundred American government agencies, educational institutions, and corporations, such as the Bechtel Corporation, General Atomic Company, Jet Propulsion Laboratories, the San Jose Police Department, and the United States Department of the Interior."[26] Having gained access to these often highly classified collections, they set to work. What they found were aging prints—most of them more than twenty years old—evidence of another time, 4 × 5 contact prints, glossy, thin official institutional images, storehouses full of evidentiary photographs, among them images of technical experiments, crime scenes, and other curiosities. As the artists explained many years later, these images were already antiquated in 1977. At that time, one might have expected to find 35-millimeter contact sheets.[27]

Building on the efforts of those who had archived and maintained these photographic collections, Sultan and Mandel become their new keepers, creating an artistic archive of their own. Their tender regard revived these antiquated pieces of evidence as art.

The idea was to cull through this vast trove of photographs, images that had been collected as official documentation—of scientific or technological experimentation and innovation, trade secrets, new procedures and protocols, even actual crime scene photographs—in order to create their art. Like Aliza Shvarts, who compiled an array of rape kits from as many states as possible, Sultan and Mandel made art out of these official photographs (see figs. 5a and 5b). Having gathered up a vast array of images, the two photographers proceeded to reshuffle them without the benefit of any context or labels. The images were decontextualized and presented anew as *Evidence*. As the artists explain, they rescued these prints from the "dustbin of history" and gave them new life. The image that opens this chapter is just one of these haunting photographs, a trace of something we can never fully know (see fig. 4).

Although these photographs had once documented specific programs, in this artistic project they lost all their instrumental value and function and instead became the stuff of connotation. Making formal connections between images, Sultan and Mandel claimed ownership of their found objects and used them to create a new narrative. They played with their fetishistic quality, allowing viewers to see the juxtaposition between their official documentary status and other, less controlled qualities, what the artists describe as "images of a loopy, odd sci-fi world" (see fig. 6). By assembling and carefully sequencing fifty-nine of these found photos, they created a kind of visual novel.[28] Or, as the American Suburb X curators explained, they were able to make "the images testify to cryptic and dubious rituals, to a culture of dehumanizing, ambiguous institutional value, to midcentury industry regarded as religion." In other words, by playing with the "documentary origins" of the photographs, the artists made them into something else entirely, without explanation. The ASX curators described the photographs as "answers to questions long ago abandoned," leaving viewers to fend for themselves, to decide for themselves what they were seeing.[29]

In many ways, I work in the spirit of this archival project. I too want to make visible that which would otherwise remain invisible. I turn not to images but rather to one of the institutional venues that Sultan and Mandel mined for their project, the police property room where "evidence" remains physically stored away and out of reach. In so doing, I also call attention to the craft, the practices that are holding or custody, and to how these labors turn objects into criminal evidence. My efforts echo not only Sultan and Mandel's project of making "evidence and its management into arts" but the work of those who hold, maintain, and serve collections in industrial and governmental archives of all kinds.

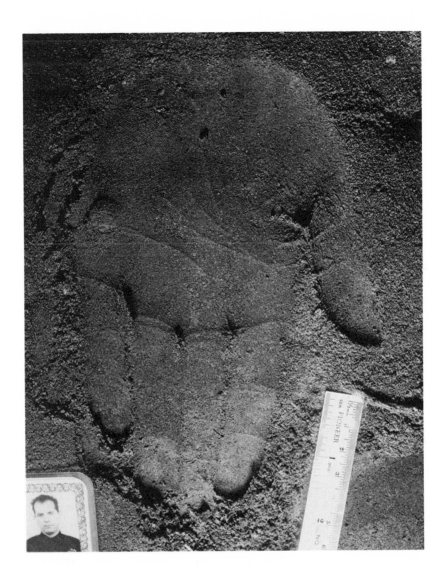

Fig. 6. Mike Mandel and Larry Sultan, *Untitled*.
From *Evidence*, 1977. © Mike Mandel, © Larry
Sultan / Courtesy of Mike Mandel and Estate of
Larry Sultan.

By focusing on those who perform these duties in such remote locations, those who make objects, like those described so meticulously by Maggie Nelson, into both sacred and evidentiary objects, I reconsider the art of custody and the allure of documentary artifacts of various kinds, objects that carry the weight of their official status as legal holdings.

The Laws of Common Usage

By focusing on the art of custody in this chapter, and on its relationship to the art of conservation in the next, I want to consider how holding, memory, and justice have been configured together for better and for worse. How do holding, memory, and justice work from the perspective of such vast and often inaccessible storerooms? What happens when we take into consideration the persons who work and the objects that live in these facilities?

Although I am concerned with the literal objects of memory, figurative objects can also prompt memory—Jane Mixer's pale blue hair band, the vast collections of beautiful objects that were once the property of the Ephrussi family, the linens and sweatpants taken from my home the night I was raped. The past, even when we are able to touch its traces, is already mediated. We come to artifacts through any number of frames and templates, explanatory stories and legends, critical theories and the works of poets and literary scholars, historians and sociologists, whose writings often introduce us to these materials in the first place. As scholars and writers, artists and lawyers, we bear the weight of their accounts. We hold and convey stories about terrible pasts and hope to approximate a sense of what they were like. And yet the pasts we transmit have not only our fingerprints on them but the traces of larger explanatory stories, what Jacques Derrida calls the "laws of common usage."[30] This notion of common usage is, in part, how we try to contain otherwise unruly stories alongside the logic of the supplement. This chapter and the next, though in different ways, both challenge the apparently self-evident explanation for why we hold on to vast repositories of pain and loss.

My fingerprints and my complicated relationship to the juridical story of my rape are all over this book. I both wanted and never got my day in court. The material record of my rape, including the rape kit, is gone.

Documentation that might show whether that kit was ever processed has also vanished. My evidence room is empty. There is only my case file, full of holes.[31]

Nevertheless, my belated encounter with the police has also helped me appreciate how much my own concerns about evidence were tied to the notion of linear justice, the law of common usage. I no longer believe that a day in court is what justice is about, at least not in my case. What I want, instead, is much closer to what both Maggie Nelson and Edmund de Waal accomplish in their writing. I want to be able to tell my story in its complexity. And the closest I could come to figuring out what happened to my evidence involved looking carefully at the rites of custody in all their detail.

My case is not special. Countless other victims of violent crimes have been left with no proof. But when there is evidence, what becomes possible?

Evidence Revisited, Berlin 2005–2006

In 2005, Larry Sultan and Mike Mandel took *Evidence*, their 1977 photographic project, to Berlin and remounted it as *Evidence Revisited*. This archival work had itself been in storage for many years and was resurrected for this exhibition. In the context of early twenty-first-century Berlin, the photographs were seen as reflecting the legacy of twentieth-century technology, bureaucracy, and social control. In 1977, as curator Carter Ratcliff explained, the images included in *Evidence* had spoken to the "utopian promise" of modern technology, even as they implicitly critiqued the very idea of technological progress. When the work resurfaced in 2005, Ratcliff suggested, it said something else: that "we are too easily seduced by the hope of total control, whether technological or social or political." Nowhere, according to Ratcliff, did the disturbing and dangerous implications of the idea of total social control resonate more fully than in the German capital: "The run-down walls in Berlin, on which *Evidence Revisited* was shown from September 2005 to June 2006, are those of a school for Jewish girls. Long in ruins, never renovated, this setting has a 'rough history,' as Sultan notes. With this understatement, he recalls the twentieth century's most atrocious attempt at social control—Nazi genocide, which made deathly use of technology."

Although Ratcliff addressed the challenges that *Evidence Revisited* posed for Berliners, he also reminded viewers that the exhibition was not an indictment so much as a provocation. It "conjur[es] up an aura," he wrote, but does not offer "solid evidence."[32] Because the photographs were not titled, viewers were asked to draw their own conclusions. We are the ones who need to keep asking questions.

The promise of all kinds of holdings is that they can be revived. I am reminded of the photograph of my sweatpants. That Sultan and Mandel's images were originally archived and then repurposed and restored as art captures one promise of custody, one that echoes not so much the logic of the supplement, as Woolf described it, but something else. It reveals the writer's own complicated relationship as an artist to the custodial labors that make possible all kinds of artistic production.

In her novel *To the Lighthouse*, Woolf writes about the temporal fragility of material objects, how things fall apart. Writing about part 2 of the novel, "Time Passes," literary theorist Maurizia Boscagli explains, "There are moments, however, when these two temporalities, the historical-human time of death, and that of the natural decay of materiality, intersect in the image of the clothes and other effects left behind by the house's occupants."[33] Although Woolf was writing more about everyday objects and not about those of industry or government, part of what she points toward is the relationship between the care of ordinary objects and the possibility of making art. "What people had shed and left," Woolf writes, "—a pair of shoes, a shooting cap, some faded skirts and coats in wardrobes—those alone kept the human shape and in the emptiness indicated where once they were filled and animated; how once hands were busy with hooks and buttons; how once the looking glass had held a face; had held a world hollowed out in which a figure turned, a hand flashed, the door opened, in came children rushing and tumbling and went out again."[34]

What is striking to me now, thinking about this image of abandoned domestic objects, is that Woolf goes on to identify the servant, Mrs. McNab, as the one who will attend to and care for these possessions. As Boscagli explains, Mrs. McNab is not quite depicted as a subject in her own right. She is, instead, aligned "with the world of things, *the* other, keeper of memory, the subject of a memory without symbol." Boscagli continues, "The objects of the past present themselves to her, as the images do to Lily. Mrs. McNab has *her* vision of Mrs. Ramsay, immediately produced by an object: 'Why, the dressing table drawers were full of things (she pulled them open), handkerchiefs, bits of ribbon. Yes, she could see Mrs. Ramsay as she came up the drive with the washing.'"[35]

Boscagli describes how Mrs. McNab's labors relate to such intimate objects: "To be aligned with objects is no natural privilege or prerogative of the humble. This representation of the subaltern is the product of Woolf's ambivalence toward 'the servants,' the ambivalence, similar to that of Mr. Ramsay, the socially minded upper-class liberal intellectual. Mrs. McNab's presence, and above all, labor, proves again that civilization is sustained by the work of the subaltern." Woolf's ambivalence illustrates how the invisible servants even in *A Room of One's Own* reflect the supplemental logic with which Woolf writes about women and history. But in *To the Lighthouse* we learn that Lily the artist cannot make art without the labor of Mrs. McNab. Not unlike Lily, Larry Sultan and Mike Mandel could not make *Evidence* without the people who initially archived those photographs. And they could not have remounted the show without the ongoing labor of those who attended to the care of those photographs in the storage facility that had housed them for decades.

"Time Passes," the second part of *To the Lighthouse*, offers an extended exploration of the impending chaos that threatens to destroy the entire world of the novel. The house is left unattended, and everything comes apart. Having imagined such entropy, Woolf describes the "restoration of order of bourgeois domesticity and reason," as Boscagli puts it. Though "willed by the Ramsays," this labor is performed by the help. It is "carried out by Mrs. McNab," Boscagli explains, "in the same way as Mrs. Ramsay had provided the recipe for the *Boeuf en Daube*, but the actual dish was cooked by Mildred. When, after ten years have gone by, Mrs. McNab sets the house in order for the Ramsays, the split temporality of 'Time Passes' is sutured by gendered human labor." Although it is not always gendered, this kind of invisible, cyclical, tedious, and necessary labor is what enables continuity over time. Objects that can move in and out of storage, packed away and returned to circulation, allow a new perspective, another interpretation. As with *Evidence* or Lily's art, the supplemental labor of custodians makes such endeavors possible. And perhaps these artistic works can help us better imagine how to tell the stories of so many other once ordinary possessions whose brush with violence has turned them into something else.

I believe that the tainted and transformed objects held in police storage facilities might be enlisted to do this more imaginative kind of work. They might help us do justice to their legacies. In a sense, creative works of art and literature are also a supplement to a juridical story that rarely gets enacted, another way of doing justice to different pasts.

Evidence Revisited asks viewers to reconsider not only the relationship between legal and industrial holdings and Holocaust memory, those mechanisms of total control, but also the relationships among collecting material evidence of crimes, the arts of conservation, and the arts of police property management that are the work of custody.

CHAPTER 5

The Arts of Conservation and Collections Management

An archival costume box in a new off-site storage facility of the United States Holocaust Memorial Museum holds a small green sweater. This handmade child's top is a piece of what the museum calls "rescued evidence" (see fig. 7). Too fragile to be on permanent display, the delicate artifact is carefully packaged and held in this temperature-controlled storage facility. The precious bequest, given to the museum by Kristine Keren, a survivor, was knitted for her by her grandmother before the war.[1] Keren wore it during the fourteen months she spent in hiding from the Nazis in the sewers of Lvov, Poland. Kristine Keren survived wearing this sweater on her body, protecting her during those horrific months.

Keren's sweater constitutes but one "rescued" piece of Holocaust evidence preserved by the USHMM and its devoted staff of conservators, curators, librarians, archivists, and collection managers. It provides an intimate reminder of all that transpired and survives as a witness to Kristine Keren's endurance, a tactile trace that connected her life before to what happened during, and after, the horrific ordeal. In a quite different storage facility in a state police barrack in Ypsilanti, Michigan, Maggie Nelson saw for the first time the cardboard criminal evidence boxes that held Jane Mixer's clothing, material evidence from the night her aunt was murdered. Nelson saw these boxes almost thirty years after that crime was committed. They were arranged on a high shelf in the office of Detective-Sergeant Eric Schroeder of the Michigan State Police, the officer in charge of the case. Out of storage, they sat alongside similar boxes,

Fig. 7. Green sweater. Photo: United States
Holocaust Memorial Museum.

all labeled with the individual names of the various young women who had been killed as part of what were known as "the Michigan Murders" (circa 1969). As Nelson explains, "the girls' names appear on the side of each box writ large in Magic Marker."[2] In *The Red Parts*, Nelson describes the contents of her aunt's boxes. She also makes clear the role of these numbered pieces of evidence in the belated murder trial. She focuses on a pair of pantyhose that contained the vital DNA evidence that broke open this cold case.

I approach questions about these kinds of holdings here from the perspective of the USHMM. But in order to appreciate how the objects in the museum's collection are cared for, we need to consider also how these two different pieces of evidence—the rescued child's sweater, a Holocaust artifact, and the pantyhose—are both similar to and different from each other.

The work of rescuing and conserving Holocaust evidence is at once like and unlike the police property management of Jane Mixer's clothing. Although in both instances the empirical data of physical evidence are collected in order to prove beyond the shadow of a doubt that terrible crimes really happened, these efforts differ markedly. Keren's sweater will never make its way to any courtroom. And yet we often engage with the juridical in relation to rescued Holocaust evidence. We do this even when there is no legal redress. I want to consider how rescuing and holding objects like Keren's sweater do a different kind of justice to the horrific past at the USHMM.

In order to examine the presumption about the legal rationale for rescuing and holding Holocaust evidence, I also want to complicate this analogy.[3] Although we often presume that Holocaust objects are like criminal evidence, what happens if we try to reverse the terms of this analogy? How is criminal evidence like a Holocaust artifact?

Holocaust collections operate outside the framework of the criminal justice system in the United States. The USHMM is not a legal repository. The evidence gathered here is not restricted to the care of criminal justice professionals, nor was it procured using the techniques required to secure criminal evidence. The sweater was a gift. There is no chain of custody and provenance is not quite the same thing that it is in criminal cases. For objects like Keren's sweater, the value of which is bound to a historical moment and not determined by some market, provenance is complicated. The determination of value in this case is difficult precisely because provenance is tied to monetary value and the history of ownership, but money is beside the point here. As an archival repository, the USHMM is by design open to the public. Its collection is meant to circulate, while criminal evidence must be restricted. It cannot be accessible.

The Art of the Invisible

Finding and retrieving are the stuff of archival, museum, library, and police collections. If these institutions are to work, they must be organized. Systems must be in place. I am reminded of Jonathan Safran Foer's account of labeled boxes in the house at the heart of his novel *Everything Is Illuminated*. Upon arrival at this place, less a house than two stuffed rooms, the narrator explains:

> One of the rooms had a bed, and a small desk, a bureau, and many things from the floor to the ceiling, including piles of more clothes and hundreds of shoes of different sizes and fashions. I could not see the wall through all of the photographs. They appeared as if they came from many different families, although I did not recognize that a few of the people were in more than one or two. All of the clothing and shoes and pictures made me reason that there must have been at least one hundred people living in that room.[4]

This is the more intimate of the two rooms, a bedroom that seems to be shared by at least one hundred people, not a single aging woman. In this space, clothing, photographs, and all those shoes are visibly on display, as if they might still be worn. This is one portion of the collection.

> The other room was also very populous. There were many boxes, which were overflowing with items. These had writing on their sides. A white cloth was overwhelming from the box marked weddings and other celebrations. The box marked privates: journals / diaries / sketchbooks / underwear was so overfilled that it appeared prepared to rupture. There was another box, marked silver / perfume / pinwheels, and one marked watches / winter,

and one marked hygiene / spools / candles, and one marked figurines / spectacles.

This is an idiosyncratic filing system indeed, and as the paragraph concludes the narrator expresses regret about not recording more of the labels. Nevertheless, he writes, "Some of the names I could not reason, like the box marked darkness, or the one with death of the firstborn written in pencil on its front. I noticed that there was a box on the top of one of these skyscrapers of boxes that was marked dust." Only by the grace of the aging woman who collected and sorted and stored, albeit precariously, all of these various items is there anything left of Trachimbrod, a town destroyed by the Nazis. And without her understanding of what lies in each of the boxes, much less all the pictures, shoes, and various articles of clothing, retrieval would be quite difficult, if not impossible.

As I read about this fictional makeshift archive, I was reminded of my own files and folders, my efforts to make order and keep track of my collected articles, drafts, notes, and other documents, which also feel precarious. The more materials we have at our fingertips, the more important it is to be able to retrieve what we want when we need it. And yet documents and notes are not the same as physical objects, which cannot be stored in computer files or ethereal "clouds." Physical objects require not only organization but—unlike computer files and folders—actual physical space. They also need to be arranged in such a way that they can be found and retrieved when they are summoned.

How can I explain this? This tension between order and disorder is very much a part of all efforts to collect and hold vital evidence of whatever kind. It is also a part of what Svetlana Boym considers in the final chapter of her book *Another Freedom: The Alternative History of an Idea*, a chapter titled "Freedom and Its Discontents." Although she takes a somewhat different tack, Boym addresses the tensions between chaos and order, the rational and the intuitive, the artistic and the quantitative, by asking us to consider Vitaly Komar and Alexander Melamid's "People's Choice" project of 1996–98. In this work, Komar and Melamid try to quantify the aesthetic and in so doing produce a work that strangely enables us to explore more fully the allure of order.[5] As Boym explains:

At the end of the cold war, Russian American artists Vitaly Komar and Alexander Melamid decided to engage, or possibly even reconcile in a paradoxical manner, Soviet and American mythologies, pledging to use a scientific method and to fulfill the promise of both Socialist Realist art and capitalist advertising. They decided to conduct an experiment: abandoning artistic freedom in the narrow sense of the word, they would instead satisfy "popular demand" and make art by the numbers, following the polls and the expression of the "people's choice."[6]

Boym goes on to describe this work; we learn that the artists "diligently conducted scientific polls of artistic tastes from Kenya to China (with the United States and Russia in between), using local teams of sociologists and statisticians who interviewed a representative population sample on all aspects of art."

In other words, using all of the tools of social science, marketing, and survey literature to calculate what art the public wanted, Komar and Melamid offered the people what they seemed to desire. The artists then presented both paintings made in accordance with what their research uncovered and a series of displays depicting the process of quantification they used in their research. As Boym explains, "Wondering whether polls are now a substitute for democratic politics and have become a new institution, Komar and Melamid made polling the main aesthetic attraction of the exhibition." People got the paintings that the numbers suggested they wanted, but they also got an account of the artists' scientific practice. "The exhibition was dominated by the ubiquitous presence of the colorful scientific graphs that resembled abstract paintings, which were just as prominently featured and on display as the 'most wanted' paintings, as if exhibiting the narcissism of polling and proceduralism for its own sake." Irony abounds in this work and in Boym's account of it. Komar and Melamid's polling found that the public wanted accessible representational art, but viewers were in fact more fascinated by the performances of abstraction, the polling on which the artists based their process, than they were by the presumably desired representational art. The process itself trumped the answers gleaned by such research. For Boym, the stakes in this work are a bit different from my own. "This project reveals ample contradictions: global versus local, democratic versus elitist, technological versus traditional, actually conspire together to create a mediocre end result that everybody 'should' want but nobody actually does. The project also confronts different logics of polls and polity, of quantitative and qualitative analysis, of democratic and artistic freedom, and offers us a phantasmagoria of the 'people's choice.'"

Perhaps this is an unusual way of thinking about the arts of conservation and collecting, but Komar and Melamid shed light on a longing for more knowledge about what goes on in the process of artistic production. They do this, strangely, after 1989, in the context of my own story. This longing crosses boundaries after the Berlin Wall has fallen. This desire for knowledge is less about artworks held in museums than about mechanisms of their procurement and processing, the labors of conservation, on the one hand, and collections management, on the other. Each, in different ways, preserves and makes possible any collection, historical or artistic, in the first place. The desire for more knowledge about process is expressed in the art of collecting—Joseph Cornell's box assemblages or the idiosyncratic form of display of the Barnes Foundation in Philadelphia, where each room is a kind of tableau, now more fully preserved in the re-creation of the original museum inside the new. At the new Barnes museum, each room is a kind of Cornell-like box with a logic of its own, demanding our attention as viewers and visitors.[7] As the Barnes architects Tod Williams and Billie Tsien explain, their work at the new Barnes was all about such containers. In 2012, for the International Architecture Exhibition at the Venice Biennale, they conceived of a project that was literally all about *Wunderkammer*.[8] Echoing the vitrines that held de Waal's netsuke, or the *Wunderkammer* of his childhood, or my own medicine cabinet, Williams and Tsien ask us to consider how holding and display, containing and preserving, are complicated, entangled desires. After all, handling such precious objects also poses dangers to their preservation. I return to these themes, and to Venice and another Biennale, in the next chapter, where I consider more fully the relationship between such containers and the precious objects they hold as contemporary reliquaries.

The work of the archive is also to keep order, to make sure that the collected holdings remain accessible. There is a kind of art and a science to this form of enactment. As I turn to the artifacts at the USHMM, I want to consider not only the public for whom this vast collection might need to be accessible but also the logic and the professional practices that keep it in order. In telling this story, I find myself in the company of many other scholars of Holocaust memory. In conversation with them, I can best explain the arts and rites of conservation and preservation at the USHMM.[9] My observations are peppered with their scholarly accounts, as they enable me to depict most vividly what takes place behind the scenes of the museum's displays.

The USHMM sees as its mission the rescue and preservation of Holocaust artifacts and related objects and making them available to the public for viewing. Although visitors to the museum want access to specific items rather than to the abstract mechanisms that make such objects available, I want to make these practices—the logic of arrangement, preservation, and retrieval not only of the objects on display in the permanent exhibit but the storage facilities that hold the vast assortment of the institution's holdings—more visible and to appreciate their artistry. The new, more public face of the USHMM's recently opened storage facility, the David and Fela Shapell Family Collections, Conservation and Research Center, anticipates not only the behind-the-scenes view of Komar and Melamid's project but my own insistence on the attraction of what happens offstage.

Rescuing the Evidence

"Rescuing the Evidence" is the tagline on the membership and donation page of the USHMM's website. The copy is succinct and to the point. On the day that I accessed this webpage, I found a family photograph of two children, a boy and girl in matching sailor suits, standing beside a Christmas tree. The photo, complete with its rough soiled edges, is surrounded by a thin black frame. The children do not face the camera directly. The boy looks toward the viewer, but at an angle. He faces the tree. He stands behind the young girl, who is seen in profile, a view that highlights the large white bow in her hair. The bow matches the bright white ties on both children. The young girl, four or five years old, stands in the foreground. We see only a few branches of the tree the children are admiring. They are decorated with ornaments. The photo credit reads:

"Gavra and Irena Mandil pose next to a Christmas tree. *US Holocaust Memorial Museum, courtesy of Gavra Mandil.*"[10] The photograph itself is a rescued remnant. Below it, the copy reads, "Every day the United States Holocaust Memorial Museum works to rescue priceless artifacts and the stories that bring them to life. This proof is essential for safeguarding truth in the face of Holocaust denial and minimization." The site goes on to ask for the public's support: "Your gift will help the Museum collect and preserve more evidence that will be used to educate future generations and help ensure the permanence of Holocaust memory."

By now, such statements are commonplace, but what do these simple words really mean? What can they tell us about the vital work of collecting and preserving such materials, the heart of the museum's mission? My Google search for "rescued Holocaust evidence, USHMM" not only took me to the USHMM donation page; it also linked me to a press release dated December 29, 2010, that read, "United States Holocaust Memorial Museum and Banca Civica Cooperate to Rescue the Evidence of the Holocaust."[11] The press release states that the USHMM and the Spanish Banca Civica entered into an agreement that allows bank "customers to help the Museum's efforts to rescue the evidence of the Holocaust. The Museum is working in more than 50 countries to rescue evidence of the Holocaust before the eyewitness generation disappears." The statement quotes the director of the museum as saying, "This collection—photographs; artifacts; films; archival documentation; testimonies from Holocaust survivors, perpetrators, and eyewitnesses; and more—will serve as a primary resource for all future generations of researchers, educators, and students studying this history." Moreover, we read, the bank will contribute to these efforts through a civic banking initiative "in which the bank discloses its earnings to its customers who then determine to distribute 30 percent of the bank's profits to a variety of non-profit organizations." Banca Civica customers can choose to support the museum through this program.

Despite the grand headline, this is a relatively small initiative. Nevertheless, the final paragraph of the press release reiterates the central aims and mission of the museum: "A living memorial to the Holocaust, the United States Holocaust Memorial Museum inspires citizens and leaders worldwide to confront hatred, prevent genocide, and promote human dignity. Federal support guarantees the Museum's permanent place on the National Mall, and its far-reaching educational programs and global impact are made possible by generous donors." The museum's collection of Holocaust artifacts enables the institution to do its work. According to this logic, visitors to the USHMM will be inspired "to confront hatred, prevent genocide, and promote human dignity" by seeing and engaging with these artifacts. By enabling the museum to continue to amass evidence, the work of educating the public will continue.

There is a kind of self-evidence to this claim, and it is powerful. I am not interested in denying such claims. Instead, I want to explore how this logic works and, more specifically, to examine the role that evidence will play in the future of Holocaust commemoration. I am concerned with how objects speak, what they can and cannot convey, and how the labors of collecting, conserving, and cataloguing inform not so much their display but their role in the USHMM's "far-reaching educational programs" especially its library, archive, and research center.[12]

Curation and Excess on Display

Through its practice of accumulation, the museum imitates the archive.
                    —Jennifer Hansen-Glucklich, *Holocaust Memory Reframed*, 128

According to *Merriam-Webster's*, a curator is "one who has the care and superintendence of something; *especially*: one in charge of a museum, zoo, or other place of exhibit." Dictionary.com suggests that a curator is a keeper or custodian of a collection not unlike a property manager in a police precinct, although I did not find this analogy in the dictionaries I consulted. Rather, they explain that in the theater, a curator selects acts to be performed, especially in musical performances, which suggests a kind of orchestration. The curator puts together the program, decides the order of the pieces, selects the objects in an array. But curate, an older noun, comes from an ecclesiological context.

We learn from Dictionary.com that the term "curator" derives from "late Middle English (denoting an ecclesiastical pastor, also [still a Scots legal term] the guardian of a minor): from Old French *curateur* or, in later use, directly from Latin *curator*, from *curare* (see cure). The current sense dates from the mid-17th cent." I do love the notion that the curator not only serves the church but also acts as guardian of a minor, according to Scots law. The term returns us to the question of custody and the labor of minding the store, or safekeeping. Moreover, the link to "cure" suggests that the person who performs these labors engages in relieving a person or animal of the symptoms of a disease or a condition. But the term "cure" is also strangely linked to a different form of preservation, as in curing meat, for example.

This second entry for "cure" says that to cure is to "preserve (meat, fish, tobacco, or an animal skin) by various methods such as salting, drying, or smoking." In this case, preservation is an act of transformation of one substance into something else, from cucumber to pickle or from one form of meat into a very different form—smoked fish, pickled herring, beef jerky, for example. And here the labors of the conservator become critical. In order to preserve, but *not* to pickle or smoke or salt the precious objects in museum collections, a special art is required, the work of conservation and preservation. A curator must work hand in hand with a conservator, whose job it is to maintain the integrity of the objects in such collections.

Curators are managers and overseers. And, I suspect, this links them in some key ways to those who labored in the church as curates.[13] They oversee the preserving of the many items in their care, with some deference to conservators, who teach us about how "curing" does not always mean "preserving."

In the context of the USHMM, the term's capacious connotations of caring, curing, attending, and orchestrating signify more than the work of the institution's curators. They speak to the labors of its various professional staff, those in charge of the collection and its upkeep—librarians, archivists, and collections managers, and, in the case of material objects, most especially the museum's conservators. As Philip Ward eloquently explains in *The Nature of Conservation*, "By definition, museums have four classic functions: they *collect*, they *preserve*, they conduct *research*, and they *present* or interpret their collections to the public in light of research." But Ward emphasizes the primacy of preservation and conservation: "*Preservation* is the most fundamental of these responsibilities, since without it research and presentation are impossible and collection is pointless. *Conservation* is the technology by which preservation is achieved."[14]

And yet conservation in this sense has only been practiced since the 1930s. It is a latecomer to the disciplines of the museum, and its tasks are so basic that they are often taken for granted, operating under the kinds of supplemental logic we have seen in the work of police property management and custodial labor—daily, cyclical tasks that sustain the integrity and maintenance of the collection.

In their important accounts of the USHMM, Oren Stier and Jennifer Hansen-Glucklich address the excess of evidence that constitutes the USHMM's permanent exhibition.[15] These Holocaust scholars summarize and expand what has increasingly become a kind of scholarly consensus on the museum and its exhibits.[16] Both pay particular attention to the central role of artifacts, noting that the logic of the museum's exhibition echoes its broader commitment to amassing and conserving as vast a collection of evidence as possible.

"The museum's permanent exhibition," Hansen-Glucklich writes, "contains approximately one thousand authentic artifacts; its overflowing displays, crammed full of photographs, objects, and texts, exemplify the idea of the museum as storehouse or repository of memory." This "excess of evidence," she says, animates the museum and its educational mission. To prove that the Holocaust happened, the museum pays especially close attention to the authenticity of its holdings. Verifiable empirical evidence is crucial; this is why authentic artifacts must be on display. The excess of such evidence marks the USHMM as distinct from other such museums and lends the institution its authority and purpose; Hansen-Glucklich observes that the USHMM's logic shares many of the display techniques common to the museums built on the sites of concentration camps, where authentic objects are central. Following Oren Stier and Edward Linenthal, among others, Hansen-Glucklich explains that in the very construction of the permanent exhibit, "the museum needed to acquire as many artifacts as possible." According to Jeshajahu Weinberg, the museum's first director, "the USHMM needed a 'terrible immensity' of artifacts." Part of what drove this desire from the beginning was the need to definitively refute the claims of Holocaust deniers, and the various statements of the museum's mission continue to emphasize this critical objective. As Hansen-Glucklich notes, "a recent upsurge in the activities of Holocaust deniers was a major reason behind the decision to include in the permanent exhibition only 'authentic materials.'"[17]

In her assessment of the permanent exhibition, Hansen-Glucklich notes that the museum's "practice of accumulation" imitates that of an archive.[18] Although this was meant as a statement about the nature of the permanent exhibition as a visible archive, it also speaks to the broader mission of the institution. And yet, as is the case in all kinds of museums, the nature of the permanent collection requires that USHMM also function as an archive. Museums often display only a fraction of their holdings, or, as in the case of the Museum of Tolerance in Los Angeles, no historical artifacts at all.[19] But at the USHMM, the displays are all about the evidence, and they are filled with artifacts. What interests me about this aesthetic of display is that it echoes directly the broader mission of the institution. But to address the USHMM's exhibition space in only these terms is to miss how the institution more consistently enacts its commitments through its collecting, conserving, and cataloguing of Holocaust evidence. The museum is not just an exhibition space. It is also a repository, a storehouse. In sharp contrast to the Los Angeles Museum of Tolerance, storage is part of its mission. And although the labor spent on this function of storage is not as overtly on display, excess is quite evident behind the scenes as well as in its public displays.

Oren Stier suggests that the museum's concern with the authenticity of the objects on display lends it a special credibility. It makes the Holocaust past manifest in the present, allowing visitors to identify with this traumatic legacy more directly. In other words, the museum's abiding commitment to offering visitors access to actual historic objects and artifacts shapes the logic of identification that the exhibit demands of its visitors. But what Stier's own work with Holocaust icons illustrates—especially the Holocaust-era train car—is just how difficult it is to authenticate such objects.[20] Empiricism cuts many ways, and the provenance of these objects can be difficult to ascertain. As everyday objects that would not otherwise be highly valued, it is quite difficult to trace their origins.[21]

Both Stier and Hansen-Glucklich suggest another reason why the USHMM offers visitors so much evidence. They argue that it helps bridge the gap between here and there, America and Europe. By removing materials from Europe and bringing them to Washington, DC, the museum shrinks this geographic distance, allowing new generations of Americans to learn about the Holocaust. Although various commentators have questioned this logic—"as if a plenum could ever speak for the enormity of this legacy,"[22] or as if, in some sense, the very removal of these objects from Europe might be read as an act of domestication, a taming and containing of the horror[23]—neither the excess of evidence nor the collection's distance from Europe ever fully succeeds.

The placement of this vast collection in the US capital promotes a different sense of safety altogether.[24] The nation's capital and the official imprimatur of the US government encourages a sense of safekeeping and permanence, especially for Holocaust survivors and their descendants, who want to be sure that the Holocaust is not forgotten. This is part of what Liliane Weissberg suggests in her provocative early account of the museum's permanent exhibition.[25]

Long ago, when I first viewed and then read about Marc Chagall's numerous paintings and glass works of Jesus, I wondered not only about their meaning but about their careful placement. I thought a lot about what it meant for this Russian-born Jewish artist to have his decidedly Jewish stained-glass windows installed at the Hadassah Medical Center in Jerusalem and also what it meant to have his Christian-inspired works built into the architecture of the Chartres Cathedral. What does it mean, for that matter, that his murals reside on the ceiling of the Paris Garnier, itself a secular cathedral devoted to the worship of high French culture? What does such placement portend for the future of the artist's work, or for his place in these seats of French heritage?[26] As with Chagall's work, I believe that the allure of the USHMM lies precisely in its presumably secure status in such a prominent location as the capital city of the most powerful nation in the world. The museum's stature as part of the Smithsonian national museum complex sends a message about the future of Holocaust memory. This institution has the backing of the US government, and the evidence held in its collections will be kept secure.[27]

As both Hansen-Glucklich and Stier point out, it is precisely because the USHMM is out of place that we can ask these questions about the evidence amassed there. The museum can function in its intended capacity because it is located far away from the European landscapes where the Holocaust took place. Part of the museum's attraction resides in the displacement of objects from Europe to the United States. As the press release about the museum's partnership with Banca Civica suggests, the museum's "permanent place on the National Mall" speaks to the desire of those who have contributed and those who will continue to contribute their precious belongings to the museum to keep its mission alive and well. Rescue and preservation are linked to power.

After visiting the museum at its opening, Liliane Weissberg eloquently expressed this desire from the perspective of a European Jew from a family of survivors. By describing the logic of the identity cards, or passports, that visitors are asked to pick up as they enter the museum, Weissberg made clear not only how she was not the intended visitor but what she sees as wrong with this practice, a strategy the museum no longer requires. For Weissberg, the historical weight of an actual passport undermined the practice.

Quoting Bertolt Brecht's statement that "the passport is the most noble part of a human being," Weissberg explains that Brecht penned these words "in response to the persecuted persons' need during the war to find a place of refuge. Real or fake or stolen, marked or unmarked with the letter 'J' for Jew, the passport was the single most desirable commodity in the thirties and forties, assuring at least the possibility of survival through escape. A passport could lead to another country or to another identity. After the war, it became a symbol of the survivor's struggle with his or her identity, or with his or her desire for assimilation."[28]

In sharp contrast to the critical importance of the passport for survivors, both during and after the Holocaust, the museum's passport can simply be taken for granted. "Whereas it was difficult to acquire a passport during the war, the museum has a more liberal approach: it offers false papers to everyone, and without question," Weissberg writes, adding that the "American seal and the Holocaust museum's logo" on the cards only underscores that they are not intended to rescue those who hold them. Instead, they act simply as a means of identification. For Weissberg, however, to take on this identification is "to become a victim, and rename myself." Originally, the idea was to have visitors check in at various stations throughout the museum to learn more about the persons on their passports, their new "identities." This system broke down, given the sheer volume of visitors, and the stations were abolished. But visitors are still encouraged to take a male or female ID card upon entering the museum, though this too, as Weissberg explains, is deeply problematic. "I take this personally, even without much encouragement," she writes. "My birth documents are false, my American citizenship acquired. Changing identities, adding passports, is nothing unfamiliar to me. But the museum does not want me to assume the sole role of victim. It asks me to be victim and victor at once. It is this latter role I may have fantasized about, but was not prepared for."[29] In recounting her complicated emotions about the power of the passport, Weissberg disrupts any smooth form of identification with victims or victors.[30]

As it turns out, identification and the carrying of such papers is much more fraught than the curators and designers of the permanent exhibition intended. The power of a US passport meant the difference between life and death; it carried an urgency that is belied by the perfunctory reenactment of the museum documents. What get lost are precisely the kinds of emotions actual survivors bring to such documentation—the promise of entry, acceptance, and protection. This is the fantasy of becoming one with the victor, in Liliane Weissberg's terms. It is also another reminder of how the museum's placement in Washington, DC, functions as a kind of safe haven for Holocaust memory.

Research Center, Library, Archive, Storage Facility

The Jack, Joseph and Morton Mandel Center for Advanced Holocaust Studies is, as its website suggests, "a high priority for the Museum." "It supports scholarship and publications in the field of Holocaust studies, promotes the growth of Holocaust studies at American universities, seeks to foster strong relationships between American and international scholars, and initiates programs to ensure the training of future generations of scholars specializing in the Holocaust."[31] One of the key components of its work is "the collection and preservation of Holocaust-related archival materials worldwide to make previously inaccessible sources available for study and new research," and it works with the USHMM's Academic Committee to facilitate such research.

The Mandel Center is the second-most public face of the museum's collection, after the permanent exhibition.[32] Through the center, the museum reaches out to scholars and teachers, inviting them to come and use its holdings. The most obvious of those holdings are its vast archival collections, which also include the resources it shares with numerous other international institutions with which it works collaboratively. These include, most significantly, the work of what was the museum's Collections Office, renamed the National Institute for Holocaust Documentation.[33] As of the summer of 2014, the museum was already combining the databases that make up its various collections, along with its library and other archival holdings.[34] The archivists, collections managers, librarians, and conservators continue to update the database, which now enables scholars and researchers to access the full range of the institution's holdings in a single system, a crucial component of the work of cataloguing and storage. Cataloguing enables the retrieval of all texts and objects stored in the USHMM's many repositories.

Because I am most interested in the material objects, which are, as we have seen, crucial to the permanent exhibition and to the museum's mission, I want to consider how these artifacts—these rescued pieces of evidence—are collected, catalogued, and preserved. The arts of conservation and preservation make up the invisible but necessary work of the Mandel Center and of the various museum professionals charged with acquiring, assessing, preserving, and conserving the museum's collection.

The Invisible Labor of Collection Management

Hair

As I began to consider more fully the holdings of the USHMM, I was haunted by the specter of women's hair shaved from the heads of camp inmates. Bales of this hair are on display at Auschwitz. This intimate, once living, embodied presence speaks to the enormity of the horror that is the Holocaust. As we look more carefully at the small sample of hair that was on loan to the museum in Washington, hair that came from the Auschwitz-Birkenau State Museum but was never displayed, we begin to appreciate the challenges that attend these human remains. As Oren Stier puts it in *Committed to Memory*, "The USHMM, in its quest to locate and display authentic artifacts as part of its museum narrative, had intended to display twenty pounds of hair on loan from the Auschwitz museum. Though this amount would not have had the 'weight' of the display at Auschwitz, it nonetheless would, one presumes, have created the desired effect."[35]

"The desired effect" would have been some approximation of the power of the bales of human hair at Auschwitz, where, as Stier explains, "nearly two-tons of hair is displayed inside an enormous glass case—pure physical presence, unmediated 'evidence of evil'" (42). The display of "women's hair shorn from camp inmates" stops Stier in his tracks, causing him to digress from his account of Holocaust icons and "the presumed sanctity of Holocaust symbols, and most especially artifacts" (41). The hair demanded that he ask different questions. And although he returned to the issue of displaying human hair at the USHMM in his later work, even in his initial account he argued that although the museum ultimately chose to represent the hair in a photograph, it nevertheless still displayed the complicated dynamics he sees as iconic. "When physical remnants are put on display—items that are actual artifacts from the time of the Holocaust, such as shoes or railway cars—the iconic mode of presentation is at its most visible. All these present themselves as unmediated effects of the Shoah, material witnesses, though mute, to the events that produced them" (41). Stier asks us to pay attention to how the context in which such objects are displayed, and the techniques of presentation that are used in these setting, inform what we experience when we encounter such artifacts. In Washington, these displays preserve "the dual import of an object at once an artifact of that time and place and a present-day image standing in metonymically for the whole to which it refers" (44).[36]

And yet the hair at the USHMM was not like those other iconic artifacts, shoes and railway cars. The stakes were different. Although the hair represented "an essential part of the story of dehumanization and commodification of Jewish bodies and had to be included in the permanent exhibition" (127), there were serious objections to its display, especially from survivors who served on the museum's content committee. As historian Edward Linenthal explains, many on the committee argued that as "fragments of human life," the hair had "an innate sanctity." It constituted a "relic of once vital individuals," and as such was better suited to a memorial and not a museum setting (127).[37] Although the USHMM was created to serve the dual purpose of memorial and museum, the sanctity of these intimate artifacts kept them from ever being put on display: in response to the objections, the museum's content committee reached a compromise: "the museum decided to install a wall-length *photograph* of the nearly two tons of human hair exhibited in Auschwitz, instead of the 'real thing.' But twenty pounds of that hair remain in a storage facility in Maryland, perhaps awaiting a time when no objections will be raised to its display" (42).

As it turned out, that time never came; the hair was never put on display. When I visited the original off-site storage facility in Maryland in the summer of 2014,[38] the twenty-year loan had ended, and the hair had been returned to Auschwitz. When I asked the museum's conservator about it, I realized that I had not fully comprehended how small a sample was in question. Of those bales of hair, the twenty pounds lent to the museum fit into just three textile boxes.[39] The hair was preserved at the offsite storage facility in those three boxes for twenty years.

As it turned out, the hair was only one of many items that the museum had to return to Poland. Not all of them, having been returned to Poland, came back to Washington again. And none of those that did return to the USHMM came back with another long-term contract. The most complicated and controversial of these lent objects was the barrack built into the architectural structure of the museum. It had to be carefully and painstakingly dismantled so that it could be sent back to Poland while a new barrack was procured and eventually shipped, unpacked, and finally retrofitted into the exhibition space.[40] Although most of these artifacts and objects, like the hair, had initially been lent to the museum for twenty years, as these contracts expired the rules for such loans also changed, and long-term loans of national historic treasures became a thing of the past. Under European Union regulations, no such objects can be on loan for more than five years. With the old contracts no longer in place, new practices and procedures had to be created to enable the museum to be in full compliance. As we shall see, this means that the shoes on display in the permanent exhibition need to be regularly sent back to Majdanek, Poland, replaced by new batches of shoes that take their place. Unlike the Torah scrolls on display in what Stier refers to as a kind of translucent casket, evidentiary relics like the boxes of hair were catalogued and accounted for but never displayed. They remained housed in an archive, out of sight but not forgotten, only ultimately to be returned to Auschwitz.

Shoes

The shoes from the concentration camp in Majdanek allow us to think through these questions from another angle, by asking what it means to display crucial artifacts that do not belong to the museum as a key component of its permanent exhibition, now that the rules around such loans have changed.

As Travis Roxlau, the director of Collections Services at the USHMM, explained to me in August 2014, the shoes are now rotated on a five-year cycle in compliance with EU and Polish government regulations. Using the services of fine arts couriers, the shoes are inventoried and a manifest is drawn up at Majdanek. The shoes are carefully counted and then boxed and crated by a fine arts courier operating out of Lublin, Poland. Once packaged and ready to go, the crates of shoes go through Warsaw customs before leaving the country. From Warsaw, the shoes are shipped to the United States via New York. In New York, the Polish couriers who accompany the package are met by the USHMM's fine arts broker. The broker takes care of the paperwork in coordination with his or her Polish counterparts. This enables the shoes to clear customs without the crates' being opened. Couriers and brokers have power of attorney that enables them to go through US customs in this special manner. The fine arts broker works with US customs to declare the shipment, again without opening the boxes. In this context, the chain of custody, the provenance of the shipment, remains unbroken. It is also worth noting that the packing of these shipments is quite delicate. For some of the objects on loan (not only the shoes), crates and mounts are custom-made for the artifacts in question, standard procedure for courier services that move valuables, especially across international borders. Items are shipped at standard rates for specialized courier services, and, needless to say, this is an expensive endeavor.

The shoes arrive at the museum via courier, still undisturbed in their crates. The packages must adjust to their new climate, which can take a week or more. Eventually, the shoes are opened in a climate-controlled environment, at 70 degrees with 50 percent humidity. The challenge is to prevent shock and condensation.

The conservator and collections management team at the museum work hard to slow the deterioration of all of the precious objects in their care. They face the challenge that, like the shoes, most of the artifacts in the museum's collection are fragile. Their value lies in their very vulnerability, the ways in which they have come to embody the horrific history of the Holocaust. The goal is to slow down "inherent vice," the properties or defects of physical objects that cause them to deteriorate owing to the fundamental instability of their various components.[41]

The shoes on display are those that were left at the end of the war, that were not repurposed, not given to the German people to reuse. Majdanek was a collection site for property confiscated by the Allies at a number of camps. This is, in part, why so many shoes ended up there. As Hansen-Glucklich explains, "the camp also served as a storage facility for victims' possessions from other camps, the shoes currently on display there belonged to victims of the killing centers of Belzec, Sobibor, and Treblinka II as well as Majdanek."[42] For many years after the war, the shoes sat outdoors in huge piles, exposed to the elements. In the 1950s, when Majdanek became a national site of remembrance, the shoes were brought in from outside and placed in a barrack in bins made of chicken wire and wooden posts. A few were sent elsewhere, but the vast majority of the shoes were kept in Majdanek. The barrack was leaky and rodent-infested and, not surprisingly, the shoes were already rotting. In the 1960s, conservators who examined them concluded that the shoes had been treated in large drums with cleaning fluid and then shoe polish. The polish hardened and cracked, creating more mold and rot. This accounts in part for the smell that accosts visitors as they enter the USHMM exhibition space where these shoes lie in open bins.[43]

Unlike works of art, or even most historical artifacts in other museums, these objects are valuable because their status is precarious. A handmade notebook that accompanied a Jewish partisan in the woods carries the stains, the wounds, of its history. It is not a pristine object, nor should it be, and the conservation of such objects requires adapting the professional standards of museum and archival practice to accommodate their particular special needs (fig. 8). This is not easy. Consider, for

Fig. 8. Diary. Photo: United States Holocaust
Memorial Museum.

example what it means to insure the shoes that travel between Lublin and
Washington, DC, every five years. What is their value? They are at once
priceless—invaluable and irreplaceable—and at the same time worthless in terms of their practical utility or monetary value. So how is their
value determined for insurance purposes? According to the museum's
chief conservator, Jane Klinger, the USHMM uses professional standards of the National Archives and Records Administration to make that
determination, specifically NARA's staff information paper 21, "Intrinsic
Value in Archival Material" (1982). The qualities and characteristics that
best describe the artifacts at the USHMM are described under number
seven, "general and substantial public interest because of direct association with famous or historically significant people, places, things, issues,
or events." Museum professionals must modify this account in order to
place Holocaust artifacts under this rubric. As the National Archives
website explains:

This criterion is not only the most difficult to apply, but also the most important in terms of the volume of records to which it could be applied. It could be used to justify preserving in original form almost all permanently valuable records because of their historical importance. On the other hand, if limited to records of unusual significance, it would be used to justify disposal of almost all original records. Archival judgment is the crucial factor in determining whether there is general and substantial public interest, whether the association is direct, and whether the subject is famous or historically significant. Generally, those series with a high concentration of such information should be preserved.[44]

Of course, not only are these criteria difficult to determine in relation to historical documents, but they become that much more complicated when applied to Holocaust artifacts. As the museum's conservator works with objects, she is bound to the standards of her profession, a profession that emerged out of the fields of art and museum studies, and she must also continuously adapt its practices.[45] The goal here is not so much to preserve objects, much less restore them to their original form. Rather, Holocaust artifacts are valuable precisely for the ways in which they were used and abused. Like the archival judge who must determine the significance of historical documents, the conservator, along with the museum's curatorial team, must assess the value of objects for this collection in unique ways. As Klinger explained to me, unlike the National Gallery or National Archives, the USHMM follows conservation and preservation practices tailored to its particular mission. Gunshot holes and stains give garments their intrinsic value, and those garments are not to be restored. The USHMM is one of the only museums in the United States that focuses on such a small slice of time. This defines the parameters of what the museum conserves. To do their work, the conservators and curators must discern the history of each particular object that comes to them, determine how it was created and how it survived. Rather than automatically "repair" the folds in a garment, they discern whether the damage is original to the period or was done after the war. This research helps the conservators authenticate the artifact and decide whether it is suitable for the museum's collection.

Fig. 9. Jane Klinger with microscope. Photo: United States Holocaust Memorial Museum.

Because much of the material in the museum's possession constitutes a form of evidence, both criminal and historical, some of the work that Klinger does resembles the labor of criminal justice professionals. Unlike that kind of work, however, the integrity of the object is central here. In order to preserve what Klinger calls "material objects of trauma," the integrity of the object is crucial.[46] As she told me, in criminal cases, the FBI generally relies on photographic evidence of the objects it holds. FBI agents often take large samples of this evidence to run their various tests. As such, their efforts often destroy the integrity of material evidence. By contrast, Klinger and her team attend carefully to the artifacts in their possession and engage in explicitly nondestructive forms of analysis. Ideally, they would refrain from taking any samples at all to do their work. It is critically important that they limit further destruction of these fragile holdings to an absolute minimum. Part of the museum's purpose is to mitigate the deterioration of such evidence.

When I described my interest in these practices to one of the librarians at the Mandel Center, he used the term "mitigation" as a way of describing such labor.[47] This is not the term preferred by the conservators, but I found it compelling. It helped me understand the broader problem of keeping Holocaust artifacts from deteriorating. He explained how textiles deteriorate. He told me to think of sewing as a violent act that automatically works to disintegrate the fabric it punctures and stitches together again. Everything in the USHMM collection is already compromised. The mandate of the conservators, collections managers, and archivists is to slow down "inherent vice," or the agents of deterioration, as much as possible (fig. 9).

Let us return to the display of shoes, which aptly demonstrates the museum's commitment to both amassing and displaying its vast collection of Holocaust artifacts. The shoes are on display en masse in a large tower space on the third floor of the museum, where, as Jennifer Hansen-Glucklich explains, they are collected in open bins "on either side of the visitors' path in a dimly lit space that is noticeably warmer than the rest of the permanent exhibition."[48] Many commentators have noted that this space is musty, permeated by the smell of hundreds of decaying shoes. The presentation is stark, the walls and ceiling, unlike the rest of the museum, made of gray concrete. There is little by way of text or explanation except for the words of a Yiddish poem titled "I Saw a Mountain," given both in Yiddish and in English translation:

We are the shoes, we are the last witnesses.
We are the shoes from grandchildren and grandfathers,
From Prague, Paris and Amsterdam,
And because we are only made of fabric and leather
And not of blood and flesh, each one of us avoided the hellfire.[49]

In her careful reading of the display, Hansen-Glucklich explains that the shoes in the poem stand in metonymically for those who died. They are "the last witnesses." The shoes do what the hair might have done, had it ever been placed on display. They bring visitors into proximity to that horrific place and time, enabling a kind of vicarious witnessing.

But the exhibit also raises questions.

The seeming self-evidence of this exhibit, its direct access to the shoes of the dead, masks the ways in which this too is a constructed space that encourages its own kind of orchestrated engagement. Despite their immediacy, these shoes cannot simply serve as witnesses of the Holocaust or the enormity of the Nazi crimes. The excess of evidence that marks the museum's larger project is made vivid in the shoes. The shoes speak to both what the museum hopes to accomplish and what it cannot.

The inescapable fact is that close proximity even to mountains of material evidence cannot offer unmediated access to the Holocaust. As scholar of Holocaust memory James Young suggests, even in the context of the actual display, the shoes of Majdanek cannot take the place of the dead. Although these remnants of the past have, in Young's words, "long come to stand in for the whole of events," all too often they are mistaken "for the events from which they have been torn." As Young makes clear, there is a danger in this logic: "in coming to stand for the whole, a fragment is confused for it. Authentic historical artifacts are used not only to gesture towards the past, to move us toward its examination, but also to naturalize particular versions of the past." The naturalization of a narrative that is far from natural is what worries Young. Despite our desire to imagine that such objects offer us unmediated access to the past, their stories are always already mediated by the narratives of the historians and collectors and curators who bring these materials into view. Young goes so far as to suggest that "museums and archives and ruins may not house our memory-work so much as displace it with claims of material evidence and proof."[50]

Even appeals to a kind of empiricism based on the historical trace are not without mediation.[51] This view of empiricism comes to us via nineteenth-century ideas that share more with the kind of allegorical logic Maggie Nelson warns against than they do with scientific proof. As Young eloquently puts it:

> The fragment presents itself not only as natural knowledge, but as a piece of the event itself. At least part of our veneration of

ruins and artifacts stems from the nineteenth-century belief that such objects embody the spirit of the people who made and used them. In this view, museum objects are not only remnants of the people they once belonged to, but also traces of the values, ideas and character of the time. In the subsequent fetishization of artifacts by curators, and of ruins by "memory-tourists," however, we risk mistaking the piece for the whole, the implied whole for the unmediated history.[52]

We risk fetishizing artifacts, granting them magical power to invoke the past of which they are only traces. And even when we know that all we have are shards, this longing seems to persist.[53]

In *Writing and Rewriting the Holocaust*, Young speaks directly to issues of representation. The past always comes to us through all kinds of narratives. And although I am less concerned about the challenge of fetishization as Young describes it, what strikes me about his account is how much the nineteenth-century legacy insists on a kind of empirical logic that is supposed to contain and perhaps tame and control the charged objects of the past. The palpable draw of such artifacts exceeds that logic or the stories we tell, which are always only our stories. The power of objects and how we engage with them is a part of numerous religious rites and practices.[54] But fetishization also suggests something else, the transitive nature of the verb *to fetishize*. We make objects into fetishes through our engagement with them. Our rituals give them power. So fetishization might be a more fruitful way of thinking about the unruly and uncontainable quality of Holocaust objects and their allure.

In her assessment of the shoe exhibit, Hansen-Glucklich challenges this empirical logic in terms of the exhibition's success. "Even more alarming than the possibility of a display failing in its efforts to bring the Holocaust 'close' is a display that, paradoxically, succeeds too well and thereby perpetuates the illusion that by accumulating enough authentic evidence, an exhibit can make the Holocaust 'knowable.'"[55] Thus one issue at stake when visitors are confronted by such historical remnants is that we believe we already know what they have to tell us. We presume that their message is self-evident. And yet, despite the language of that Yiddish poem, and as these commentators all suggest, it is crucial to remember that the shoes on display are ultimately mute. The poet and the curators attempt to make the shoes into witnesses. And yet alone they can never offer unmediated access to the Holocaust.

Contemporary Relics: No Easy Conclusions
According to historian of material culture Leora Auslander:

> Even the objects used in everyday, repetitive embodied activities, such as eating or grooming (to say nothing of ritual objects) are not simply functional; they are always also modes of communication, or memory cues, or expressions of the psyche or extensions of the body, as well as sites of aesthetic investment, involving pleasure, distress, or conscious indifference. Their makers and users understand them to have special attributes not only because of their contact with the human body, but because they themselves mirror two crucial characteristics of human existence. They, like the people who use them, are embodied. That embodiment means that objects occupy space and cannot be in two places at once, and they are mortal, although their life-spans may be much longer or shorter than those of the people who use them.[56]

Clearly, the material remains held and carefully displayed at the USHMM are deeply compelling. They are crucial to the logic of the museum and its mandate to "rescue evidence" and accumulate as many objects as possible. The evidence is proof that the Holocaust happened, and it keeps the memory of Nazi atrocities alive. Like the objects Auslander describes, these artifacts are not simply functional. These once everyday objects operate as "modes of communication, or memory cues." The law of common usage shifts. Not only do "their makers and users understand them to have special attributes," but museumgoers who see them on display and scholars who seek them out at the museum's research center, archive, and library also appreciate their "special attributes."

Moreover, the fragility of these holdings complicates their deployment as juridical or historical evidence. This evidence must be attended to, cared for, conserved. The delicate care that they require is more akin to the sacred labor of early conservators whose job it was to attend to sacred relics.

In an essay for a forum on the question of "evidence" in the study of North American religion, Jennifer Hughes writes, "Many of the Meso-american traditions that I study . . . share a common religio-affective posture of tender regard for mundane objects imbued with life: maize plants, mountains, stones, divine effigies and 'idols,' ancestral bundles, and (since the colonial period) saints' images. All of these objects are engaged as sacred persons; as 'beings' not 'things.'" She continues, "The religious objects under consideration here are better comprehended, first and foremost, as vital, dynamic, and even agentive members of the communities that we study. They are material manifestations of the sacred, to whom devotees and practitioners attribute *animus*—existence, being, desire, and potency. They possess a 'vital materiality.'"[57] Following Hughes, I want to suggest that the rescued Holocaust artifacts in the USHMM collection are similarly animate.

While acknowledging that many scholars bristle at such a claim,[58] Hughes insists that sacred objects are not passive vessels to be used for some other purpose, as the terms "fetish" and "animism" presume. For her, such "object-entities" are not narrowly, and certainly not exclu-sively, "evidence" but are "active participants in the complex religio-social networks that ethnographers of religion observe and describe." Objects performing as evidence, she says, "do so through the 'prerogative of power.'" Like Hughes, I am interested in deploying "vital materialist ontologies" in order to "better attend to these dynamic actors."[59] I want to appreciate the ways in which Holocaust objects are not exclusively "evidence" but rather vital actors in the work of commemoration.

Visitors to the USHMM stare numbly at a display of hundreds and hundreds of shoes. The individual stories of their owners, though lost, collectively yet quietly cry out. Individual objects, like Kristine Keren's green sweater, draw us into the presence of the personal horror of the Holocaust. A single shoe from the shoe exhibit, likewise, can grip us with a vicelike awareness that a real person wore those shoes.[60] Such objects both collectively and individually move us toward understand-ing. Having offered an eloquent account of the power of such objects as "the Holocaust's residue" and of how they stand in for all those whose lives remain little known, Liliane Weissberg tells this story in her 1999 essay:

> Miles Lerman, national campaign chairman for the museum, recalls the transfer of artifacts from Poland in one of his fund-raising letters: "I was asked to pose for a photograph with one of these items—a child's shoe. Let me tell you, when this little shoe was handed to me, I froze. Bear in mind that I am a former partisan. I was hardened in battle and I deal with the Holocaust story almost on a daily basis. But when I held in my hand that shoe—the shoe of a little girl who could have been my own granddaughter—it just devastated me."

The museum wants to repeat this kind of encounter. It hopes that shoes like this might "aid identification and bridge the time," as Weissberg puts it. But visitors to the museum do not encounter a single shoe. They are confronted by hundreds of shoes. The "sheer number of shoes, a fraction of the surviving pairs found in Auschwitz . . . give evidence of the enormity of the crime. These were shoes sorted by prisoners once their owners had been selected for the gas chambers, but they were not used again: sandals, walking shoes, children's slippers."[61] The shoes on display have become something else entirely. Like an exhibit of artworks, they do and they do not actually offer visitors access to those who once wore them, touched them, or tied them.[62] "The shoes in the Holocaust museum offer and resist to give such information," Weissberg writes. "They have turned into a uniform gray, a color that masks their individual shapes. Once worn by living human beings, they are now evidence of their deaths. Unique and homogenized into a pile."[63]

This tension haunts the logic of the museum, its permanent exhibition and its vast collection, at once unique and homogenized. A single shoe or a child's green sweater might pierce us deeply, especially if we could actually hold it in our hands. But the vastness of the display of so many now graying shoes prohibits such intimate identification. Nonetheless, the museum continues, even more urgently now than when it first opened and Liliane Weissberg wrote those words, to look for individual stories as a way to keep the power of such object-entities alive. They are the touchstones, the prompts for ongoing engagement with this past.

As the Holocaust grows more distant in time, the work of the museum's curators increasingly involves collecting artifacts. "In 50 countries across six continents, the Museum is aggressively collecting evidence of the Holocaust before it is too late—before fragile documents and artifacts disintegrate and while those who can bear witness are still able to do so. The Museum collection is the foundation for ensuring the permanence of Holocaust remembrance, research, and education." As noted above, this mission is directly connected to resisting Holocaust denial. "With the rise of Holocaust denial," the statement concludes, "the power and authenticity of our collection assumes ever greater urgency."[64] The museum encourages Holocaust survivors and other donors to consider placing their deeply personal possessions in the museum's collection for safekeeping, for posterity.[65]

As we have seen, these efforts are vividly on display in the museum's online art and artifacts exhibition, *Curators Corner*, and now a sample of such stories is a part of the video about the new storage and research facility, aptly titled *Safeguarding Truth Forever*.[66] *Curators Corner*, the museum's open-access video, narrative, and photographic exhibition, offers the public access to these often profoundly vulnerable objects, along with their owners and their individual stories. This is how I first learned about Kristine Keren and her sweater. Thanks to the internet, the museum can do this virtually, without tampering with the integrity of the artifacts. By allowing the objects to remain carefully in storage, the virtual display requires little actual handling. The museum can safeguard rescued pieces of evidence from the wear and tear of physical display.[67]

The collected shards held in all kinds of storage facilities have many stories yet to be told. This telling is a part of what it means to do justice to these pasts and keep these legacies alive. This form of sacred engagement is a kind of doing justice that happens beside or alongside the criminal justice system. By sharing these stories in all kinds of ways, we begin to participate in the kind of diasporic intimacy that Svetlana Boym describes.

Although Jane Mixer did not bequeath her pantyhose to the Michigan State Police, they, like Kristine Keren's sweater, tell a story. In her niece's hands, Mixer's pantyhose help Maggie Nelson give new life to the story of Mixer's life and her death. Taken as a legal exhibit and kept in storage for the purpose of going to court, they performed in one way, but in Nelson's texts they became part of a different form of doing justice. They helped Nelson tell a more complicated story. By contrast, Kristine Keren placed her childhood sweater in the collection of the USHMM for safekeeping. This sweater will never make its way to court. But it has enabled Keren to tell part of her harrowing story of survival, via the USHMM. Through the *Curators Corner* exhibit, Keren offered a different kind of testimony. In her own words, she breathed new life into that tattered sweater. This is something Jane Mixer was never able to do.

CHAPTER 6

Tending to Sacred Objects and Their Afterlives

We may be able to live without certainty. But can we really live without wonder?

—Andrea Nightingale, "On Wandering and Wondering," 53

After I was raped, I could not imagine how I could ever reclaim the sacred in my own life. Having rejected the temptation of religious answers, I reached for logic, for empiricism, for claims to hold on to, as if I could ever have that much control. Bound by a desire for certainty, I held tightly to the promise of evidence. In leaving what I knew as religion, I was participating in what classicist Andrea Nightingale describes as "the valorization of certainty and the demotion of wonder."[1] But that was not what I found, nor is it the logic of this book. Instead, in writing about the afterlives of objects, I have discovered the sacred all around me, the magic and wonder that never went away.

Even in my most negative and hopeless moments while writing this book, I found myself struck by coincidences, unexpected connections between the objects and the practices I was writing about. Just after reading *The Red Parts* for the first time, while at a conference titled "No Direction Home," I returned to my hotel room and turned on the television, only to hear Maggie Nelson's voice. It was the episode of *48 Hours* devoted to Jane Mixer's case.[2] It felt like a sign that I was on the right track, and I kept going. Svetlana Boym calls this form of connection "diaspora intimacy," noting that it can only be approached indirectly.

I spent much of the summer of 2018 editing chapters 2 and 3. Returning to those drafts, I began to see more clearly how I had allowed myself to get lost in their words. I was drawn to *Jane: A Murder*, *The Red Parts*, and *The Hare with Amber Eyes* because they told the kinds of stories I longed to write. I needed to get as close as I could to those texts to figure out how they worked. I was with their authors word by word as they tracked down their stories. They gave me a way to begin to track my own. In those draft chapters, I kept company with them.[3] I was figuring out slowly, unconsciously, how these texts were bringing me back to my own story.

Religion as Material Practice

What are the obstacles that get in the way of our claiming the sacred qualities of everyday life and the objects all around us? Why is it so difficult to embrace them?

By drawing connections between inanimate objects and a sense of wonder, I claim a different, more immanent form of religion. We participate in rituals of tender regard for objects, and these rituals have a magic with its own logic. Object-entities like Jane Mixer's jumper, my sheets, or that blue-and white-striped prisoner uniform in storage at the USHMM cry out to us.

Touch and critical engagement keep these object-entities alive, allowing them many afterlives. They infuse even the physical containers that hold and preserve them—evidence boxes and all kinds of vitrines—with their animating energy. Relics hold this power and it's how they remain relevant. Instead of trying to confine this energy, rituals of conservation and holding only add to its allure. Although many scholars are embarrassed by these seemingly superstitious beliefs, I want to push against this discomfort.

When I first presented this material at a comparative literature conference, I was surprised by the disdain my paper provoked from the panelist designated to respond to it. For him, either all objects were animate and meant nothing, or no objects were animate and meant nothing. There was no in-between, no both/and position. The argument for animate objects was completely inconsistent with this person's commitment to a more rational worldview.[4]

As a scholar of religion, I was well aware of a discomfort with religious expression in other fields of the humanities, but I had not expected this dismissive response to my work. Evidence presumes our power over the objects we write and think about. My insistence on recognizing their agency challenged this desire for control. This scholar belittled my interest in the irrational, the magical, and the wondrous. For him, such unenlightened commitments and beliefs belonged outside of the realm of scholarship. I disagree.

Having brought together an idiosyncratic array of objects and stories, practices and institutions, I want to reconsider some of the prohibitions and discomforts that arise when objects are removed from their familiar settings and the stories that once explained them. I turn to what art historian Alexander Nagel describes as the afterlives of reliquaries to talk about sacred objects and how we hold them.[5] Building on Nagel's work, I use the language of relics and their containers to explore the sacred nature of the evidence and the archives at the heart of this book. This discourse brings us full circle, a return to the medieval—and contemporary—attraction to bloody garments and the lively afterlives of all of these objects, their containers, and the places that hold them.

Unruly Objects

Throughout this book, I have wrestled with what it means to make unruly objects into something more familiar and knowable, to make them participate in what Jacques Derrida has called the "law of normal usage," a law that often effaces the very disruptive nature of such artifacts.[6] Tainted objects held as "evidence" are no longer bound by one version of common usage and are quickly taken up into another. They move from clothing to be worn to legal exhibits, but what about wonder, or the process of fetishization that James Young worries about? How do we account for the unruly qualities of Jane Mixer's clothing, or the bins of shoes at the USHMM? Once "unbound," clothing and footwear become not just criminal evidence but also, at the same time, often holy. This contradiction creates the alchemy that makes the shoes so compelling. Their attraction exceeds their presumed function. They are evidentiary, talismanic, and sacred. Their smell, their specificity, is not unlike the object-entities[7] revered by all kinds of religious cultures. They have become contemporary relics,[8] at once priceless and worthless, transformed by their proximity to violence.[9] The labors of the custodians and conservators keep them alive, and they are resurrected in a different way by poets and artists like Maggie Nelson and Edmund de Waal, Larry Sultan and Mike Mandel. We need to reconsider the stories we tell about these artifacts and the practices that define our relationships with them, the normal and extraordinary narratives that explain their meanings, stories that keep changing.

Why hold such objects? What does it mean that their import is not simply subsumed under the teleological logic of either the law or a form of historical empiricism? The logic of gathering these artifacts to serve as evidence, proof positive, that terrible crimes were committed does not encompass all that these sacred objects mean or what they do. Nor does this logic explain their care.

Animate Objects: The Return of the Dismissed

Some scholars suggest that the disdain for holy objects dates back to when "Europe rejected objects that were attributed with animating powers."[10] These scholars describe an abiding discomfort with both the African fetish and the "true spiritual power of relics, indulgences, and sacraments." Like the panelist who dismissed my work, Dutch Protestants in the seventeenth century linked Catholic and Akan beliefs in animate objects together, making them both into forms of "demonized idolatry." In many ways, contemporary academic scholarship is the heir to those Dutch Protestants, precursors to enlightened rational Western subjects, the very people who saw themselves as proper Europeans, "unconstrained by the constituting power of objects."[11] These are some of the historical antecedents for a whole series of lingering kinds of discomfort around all kinds of objects, objects whose allure exceeds the stories we tell about them.[12]

Part of historian Peter Novick's critique of the Holocaust in American life is also built on such assumptions. His position highlights a swath of scholarship and uses the Holocaust to make his case. In his important study, Novick positions himself as a secular critic of the sacred rites of Holocaust commemoration.[13] He dismisses these enactments as religious while also disparaging them for being specifically Christian.[14] He uses these claims to challenge their Jewish authenticity.[15]

In his introduction, Novick writes that guarding memories of the Holocaust is in keeping with Jewish tradition: "certainly, forgetting the Holocaust—hardly an option—would be contrary to tradition."[16] He cites historian Yosef Hayim Yerushalmi, the author of an important book on Jewish memory, *Zakhor: Jewish History and Jewish Memory*, to remind readers of the 169 instances of the verb "to remember" in the Hebrew Bible (10). This makes these enactments somehow legitimately Jewish. But according to Novick, what the biblical text commands Jews to remember is "almost always God's handiwork; secular history, insofar as such a category is even admitted by the tradition, gets short shrift" (10). This is a false dichotomy, and yet it is the linchpin of Novick's argument. Having explained that it is a Jewish obligation to mourn and remember the dead (10), he explains, "Judaism has consistently disparaged excessive or overtly prolonged mourning" (10–11), and he reminds readers that cremation is prohibited "because it would dispose of the body too soon," while embalming is prohibited for the opposite reason, "because it would preserve the body too long" (11). He says that Jews are to mourn, but not too much. They need to move on, to "choose life" (11).

Novick then turns to the other side of his argument. "One of the things I find most striking about much of recent Jewish Holocaust commemoration is how un-Jewish—how *Christian*—it is" (11). Having clarified this claim, he goes on to describe the most objectionable versions of this form of commemoration.

I am thinking of the ritual of reverently following the structured pathways of the Holocaust in the major museums, which resembles nothing so much as the Stations of the Cross on the Via Dolorosa; the fetishized objects on display like so many fragments of the True Cross or shin bones of saints; the symbolic representations of the Holocaust—notably in the climax of Elie Wiesel's *Night*— that employ crucifixion imagery. Perhaps most significantly, there is the way that suffering is sacralized and portrayed as the path to wisdom—the cult of the survivor as secular saint. These are themes that have some minor and peripheral precedent in Jewish tradition, but they resonate more powerfully with major themes in Christianity. (11)

Resisting this account in this context, I am struck by a number of things. First, the idea that these practices are "minor and peripheral" in terms of precedent in Jewish tradition is itself a complicated argument. Despite his claims to the contrary, Novick here admits that these practices are a part of Jewish tradition. I am reminded of the medieval figure of the *porphyrion* of God covered with the blood of Jewish martyrs. Nevertheless, it is as if by marking these engagements as Christian that they become, by definition, un-Jewish and unacceptable. This is, of course, in sharp contrast with the ways that Miki Kratsman embraces a Christian reverence for relics to call attention to the suffering of Palestinian martyrs, or my own efforts to reclaim a more immanent form of religious expression here.[17]

This Jewish/Christian dichotomy in Novick's text is like the distinction between the religious and the secular, the other opposition that shapes his critique. Here, Novick deploys the kinds of modernist supersessionary binaries that religious studies scholar Sally Promey points to in her work on sensational religion: "sacred/secular, image/word, concrete/abstract, material/immaterial, exterior/interior, sensation/cognition, body/mind, emotion/reason, belief/knowledge, nature/culture, particular/universal." In Novick's account, the religious enactments, which constitute one side of these oppositions, are anachronistic. They echo medieval religious practices and as such are unacceptable. As Promey explains, "What most clearly distinguished 'primitive' peoples, practices, and times was their 'superstitious' attachment to objects as fetishes and idols, their willingness to ascribe agency or other sorts of power to them, to allow them to present and mediate the supernatural."[18] This is what Novick finds so objectionable about Holocaust commemorative practices. For him, they are not Jewish but atavistic, a throwback to some pre-enlightened form of religious expression and embarrassingly not secular.[19] And yet he acknowledges their pervasive presence.[20]

I also worry about making suffering itself redemptive. Yet at the same time, the profound and relentless pain and mourning that Holocaust survivors experience haunt me. Do these relics and rituals serve a legitimate purpose? Yes. They continue to dramatize this legacy. The afterlives of Holocaust objects help us make meaning as they transform the profane into the sacred.[21]

Even if these rituals are peripheral Jewish practices of commemoration, they are still very much a part of the tradition. They cannot be so easily dismissed. So instead of turning away, instead of mocking these antiquated, atavistic rituals, especially the reverence for "fragments of the True Cross or shin bones of saints," I want to appreciate the work they continue to do and what they illuminate about our collective longing to mourn, to pay respect and remember catastrophe, and the future of such commemoration. Although these are the kinds of practices "Western modernity formerly claimed to discipline and subdue," I share Sally Promey's interest "in the ways practices resist and exceed ideology, offering new avenues forward."[22]

Housing Afterlives

The logic of the reliquary, of holding and housing fragile evidence, occasions the creation of new containers. Here is just one example. For *Reporting from the Front*, the Fifteenth International Architecture Exhibition at the Venice Biennale in 2016, Robert Jan van Pelt and his team from the University of Waterloo returned to the forensic evidence Van Pelt had gathered at Auschwitz-Birkenau. These forensic documents were originally gathered to challenge the claims of Holocaust denier David Irving. Van Pelt used them as a key witness in the 1996–2000 Deborah Lipstadt libel trial (the subject of the 2016 film *Denial*, starring Rachel Weisz).[23] In Venice, they became the basis for Van Pelt's contribution to the Biennale.

The Waterloo team used copies of those documents to reconstruct what Van Pelt had found in the archive. They painstakingly re-created that material in three dimensions and produced what they called *The Evidence Room*, an architectural exhibit where, as Holocaust survivor Elly Gotz explained, visitors were able to touch this past. "Most people know about the Holocaust. It is possible to know things, to be aware of them, but not feel them. This exhibition lets people touch the metal of the gas column, run their fingers over the drawings, and connect in that mysterious way that sometimes happens when reality overwhelms us by becoming part of us." By casting the documents at the heart of Van Pelt's testimony in plaster, the team made these texts tactile. They became the walls that revolved around key reconstructed elements of that lost architecture of destruction, the door to the gas chamber and the gas column—"the double grates that protected the bucket filled with poison pellets."[24] They used the designs, the specifications from those documents, to rebuild these pieces.

And so it was that in 2016 not only did the film *Denial* revive and revisit this case about Holocaust memory and the historian's role in verifying "historical facts," but *The Evidence Room* gave new life to Van Pelt's testimony. This painstaking forensic exhibition was an evidentiary reliquary.

I went with my friend Ruth Ost to Venice to see *The Evidence Room* as it initially stood within the vast exhibition hall of *Reporting from the Front*. I needed to see it. In this newly constituted space of memory, I experienced a different way into the ethics of housing traumatic memory. As we discovered, the Biennale is itself a kind of reliquary.

This is one of the ways in which we house the afterlives of objects. But what do relics and reliquaries teach us about such efforts? Like the forensic documents that we can touch in *The Evidence Room*, relics are often housed in beautifully crafted containers. They are held in vast storage facilities, ephemeral exhibitions, and private collections. In these venues, they are displayed in various smaller containers. These are similar to the vitrines that held de Waal's netsuke collection or the medical cabinet that holds my pottery. These are both a form of reliquary.[25]

Contact between relics and the materials that brush up against them—that wipe and polish, display and contain them—is transformative. Touch animates these objects. By virtue of their proximity to sacred shards, the containers become secondary relics. In other words, the reliquary itself participates in the ongoing life of the relic it houses. In this way, the architectural space that Van Pelt and his team created is a tactile sacred space. This became clearer to me when I visited the exhibit again in Toronto, where I got to spend time with Robert Jan van Pelt. And it was only there that I realized that visitors were welcome to actually touch the casts and reproductions.[26]

The ritual acts, the performative labors of conservation and custody in *The Evidence Room*, like the photographs in Sultan and Mandel's *Evidence*, make and remake or repurpose that which has been stored.[27]

In the book that accompanied the exhibition, Anne Bordeleau, the architect and historian in charge of making the casts of all the archival records, writes of *The Evidence Room*, "It displays drawings, constructions, and artifacts as intentional productions, indexes pointing to the hands that made them. It strips architecture of its mundane veil and reveals it in its bleakest light" (118). When the artists cast the Holocaust documents in plaster, visitors at the Biennale were able to touch the traces of death.

Writing in the catalogue for a major contemporary exhibit of sacred art at the British Museum, *Treasures of Heaven*, Alexander Nagel explains, "The display of relics typically assumed a nested structure: reliquaries were kept inside larger housings, and these were placed in structures that functioned both as buildings and macro-reliquaries."[28] These holders are both beautiful and bleak.[29]

The curators who produced *Treasures of Heaven* for the British Museum worried that visitors would want to touch the sacred objects on display.[30] This is the kind of tactile longing *The Evidence Room* embraced as a reliquary.

In his essay in the catalogue, "The Afterlife of the Reliquary," Nagel speaks to the history of collections in Venice. Describing the Gualdo Collection assembled in the sixteenth and seventeenth centuries, a collection full of relics, including pieces of the True Cross, he explains, "More than simple containers for the sacred, reliquaries were multiple structures worthy of attention as *curiosa* in their own right."[31] Venice has a long history of reverence for reliquaries. The links between Venice, containers, rooms, and memory also seem to have shaped Van Pelt's vision for *The Evidence Room*.

Inspired by his mentor Dame Frances Yates, author of *The Art of Memory* (1966) and *Theatre of the World* (1969), who introduced him "'to the concept of a building as a vessel of memory'" (79), Van Pelt hoped to accomplish in *The Evidence Room* what was "most perfectly exemplified in Giulio Camillo's Theatre of Memory, a room filled with images that allow the visitor to 'at once perceive with his eyes everything that is otherwise hidden in the depths of the human mind'" (79). That memory palace had its own historical relationship to Venice, enabling Van Pelt to return to his teacher and that memory room to conclude his essay. Writing from his studio in Canada in February 2016, amid the collection of all of "the elements of *The Evidence Room*, which will come together in Venice," he tells readers that Camillo's Theatre of Memory was also "a temporary installation" and "for the few months that it existed, five centuries ago, it too stood in Venice" (86). Addressing the longer history of Venetian reliquary art, Nagel writes, "Museological commemoration was thus layered over the cult of relics, sometimes even on the sites of religious foundations. During the French invasion of Italy, the Venetian priest Guglielmo Wambel scrambled to save the sacred objects of Venice, amassing a collection of close to ten thousand items, including thousands of reliquaries, which shortly after his death were installed in a newly built rotunda attached to the Church of San Toma. Although still in a cult-setting, this new construction was just as importantly a proto-museum of religious art."[32]

All of these containers were preserved and displayed on sacred ground. They were containers within containers, another iteration of the *Wunderkammer* at the 2012 Biennale, described in chapter 5.[33] The Biennale's vast venues house a full array of nested reliquary objects, each a carefully crafted installation in and of itself. But, like *The Evidence Room*, these layered pieces call attention to the workmanship and art of their creation. Provocative, compelling, and often beautiful architectural containers, they manifest the rituals of creation and conservation. The pavilions and exhibition halls of Venice remain standing, even as they are refurbished and reconstituted piece by piece each year as art and architecture.[34]

Living with Wonder, Criminal Justice, and the Hand of God

In a late chapter of *The Red Parts*, Maggie Nelson describes in detail visiting the Michigan State Police post in Ypsilanti where she met with Detective Schroeder, the officer in charge of her aunt's case. She describes seeing for the first time the containers that held the DNA (the pantyhose, the hair band, the jumper, the paperback book), all of the crucial evidence in the state's case. It was all there in cardboard evidence boxes on a high shelf above Detective Schroeder's desk.[35] She sees the labeled boxes from each of the Michigan murder cases, writing, "It feels like the last scene of *Raiders of the Lost Ark*, when the all-important, destructive, and sublime ark has been crated up, and a whistling janitor is wheeling it into an enormous warehouse of identical crates, unwittingly resubmerging its mystery" (185).

But these labeled boxes come from a different kind of storehouse. They hold an infinite amount of pain and loss. These are the kinds of boxes I have longed to find in my own case. "God only knows what these boxes hold—what 'cellular deposits' yet to be decoded, what flakes of dried blood, what ensembles of clothing, what other arbitrary and wrenching mementos from these girls' bodies and lives," Nelson writes (185).

Nelson's chapter is titled "The Hand of God," because this is how Detective Schroeder thinks about his relationship to Jane and to this case. "Jane's ghost has come to him in the middle of the night." He believes that Jane has "come back to transform—even to save—his life, in addition to guiding his investigation." According to Schroeder, "all matters related to Jane's case . . . are being directed by 'the hand of God'" (186). The detective works his case, acknowledging a sense of wonder, something working the case beyond logic. That force and his painstaking labor are both in play. For this detective, it is a sacred endeavor. With a fierce humility, he forges ahead. And although there are, in his view, two hands engaged in these labors, they do not constitute a pair. They work with and sometimes against each other, offering, now and then, just a little justice leavened with some company. This is the promise of the exceptional case. Even when the legal system is doing its best, justice remains elusive. But for those of us without evidence, without any leads, with no hope of a reopened case or such boxes, what is there to hold on to? The hand of God becomes that much more compelling. Its imprint on our talismanic evidence accompanies us into an uncertain future, helping us make the brutal tender.[36]

I thought I could count on logic and empiricism to comfort me. There was no reason I should have checked the back door. The rape, therefore, was not my fault. This tidy logic, though, was not enough. The detective working Jane Mixer's case understood that his investigation had a dimension beyond logic, something he called the hand of God. I cannot call it that. But his articulating that there was something beyond his control allowed a space for me to have compassion for myself. This something else does not replace uncertainty, but it does leave a space for wonder and compassion. Looking at sacred objects, and especially processing the prose of Nelson, de Waal, and Detective Schroeder, I have learned to live without certainty. But I cannot live without wonder.

Coda
Returning to Atlanta, Carrying On

November 2015, just before Thanksgiving. I am visiting Atlanta for a conference, and my partner, David, and I decide to take an extra day to unwind. We are off to visit the High Museum on Peachtree Street. As we emerge from the MARTA station, I am disoriented. I recognize the museum's stark lines and the curves of the white-walled complex, but they have been transformed. And where is Peachtree Street? Where is the front entrance to the museum? I can't figure out how these once familiar landmarks relate to the museum's white walls. We follow the signs and enter a new space. None of this is familiar.

It's a beautiful day. We leave the museum, walk to Peachtree, and head toward the Margaret Mitchell House off 10th Street. When I lived in Atlanta, the house was a mere shell. Today, it's a fully restored historical museum. We take pictures for David's mother and purchase a few postcards. We decide that a walk is in order.

I explain to him that I want to see my old house, which is nearby. We walk down 10th Street toward the park. So much has changed. I am relieved to see that Blake's, the gay bar, is still on the park.

The first house I see is the 1920s bungalow glass house, where I stayed just after I was raped. This was where I first brought my new rescued golden retriever, Bleiben. My potter once lived there. Just around the corner stands my old house. On this bright, warm day, the large plate glass windows at the front of the house shine. And is that an addition, another floor above what I remembered? Maybe I have simply forgotten this part of the house, but I am pleased to see it, sitting high and noble above the sidewalk. I had forgotten that visitors must walk up a steep incline and a number of stairs to get to the front door.

What was once my house also sits on the high side of 9th Street. The houses across from it were often flooded by heavy rain. I remember that one of those lower-standing houses once caught fire. I became a believer in at least one public institution, the fire department. Firefighters saved the house, and long ago I watched them do it.

As we turned the corner and walked that first block, I didn't know what to expect. It had been about ten years since I last visited this place. Even then, it looked about the same as I remembered it.

More than fifteen years ago I was there with my friend Miriam. We went around the block to see the backyard, carrying a trowel and a packet of seeds, part of a ritual of renewal we planned to undertake. The open yard was untouched. At that time, the screen door and the back porch were exactly the same as they had been. The screen that had been cut by the rapist was still an open wound, just as it had been, slit. We planted the flower seeds along the property line just next to the alley.

Now, however, the house is transformed—the red brick 1920s duplex, a stately symmetrical structure, is no longer red. The side porches on both floors have been made into rooms, tastefully bricked in, as if they had always been this way. The house is now an elegant gray, with black accents along the windowpanes. The yard is enclosed and there is a gray structure that seems to stand close by in the back as you look up at the house from the street. Once we go around the block and enter the back alley, it becomes clear that the gray structure is a large garage with an apartment above it. This garage stands where we used to park our cars.

Toward the other side, close to where Miriam and I planted those seeds, there is now a fence. It encloses a tasteful small swimming pool, a patio, and a small swath of grass. This area is much smaller than the full grassy yard my landlady diligently mowed each summer when I lived in this house. Even as a frail older woman, she lugged that contraption, an old-fashioned push-mower, out of her basement regularly to keep the lawn just so.

As I let myself look more closely at the back of the house, I realize that the back porch, that rickety structure where I hooked up a mustard-colored washer and dryer I inherited the last year I lived in Atlanta, that same space where the rapist cut his way into my house, is no longer there. Not a trace. This too is now bricked in. The back of the house is smooth. I realize as well that there is no longer a stairwell leading up to the second-floor apartment where my landlady lived. This is more evidence that the house has been fully gutted and remade into a single-family dwelling.

I do not know what I expected to see, but it was not this. I do not know how to express my strange pleasure at seeing this house transformed. The house of pain has become something else. And it is beautiful. I am so unnerved by this transformation that later that night, back in our hotel room, I pop out of bed in the middle of the night in order to double-check. I google the address and check it against the address as I wrote about it in my first book. It's the same place.

In Atlanta, twenty-six years after I was raped, I realized that it was almost a lifetime ago when I first moved into that house. I was twenty-seven years old when I entered graduate school, twenty-nine when I was raped. Now, approaching fifty-six, I struggled to imagine how much time had passed. I thought of my first visit to Berlin in the spring of 2014. On that visit, I searched for signs of life before the Wall came down in November 1989. In Atlanta, I thought again about contemporary Berlin and the changes in that city and its structures—walls come down, new buildings go up, what was destroyed is remade. And writing this now, I struggle not to resort to clichés. It is all so overdetermined: that glass house in Atlanta is where I watched that other Wall come down. Could it have been that long ago?

I was not, in the end, able to meet with anyone from the Atlanta police in November 2015. As I began writing this book, I also googled "911 problems, Atlanta, Douglas Lavin" to see if I could find the article about my rape, but the only reference to that article on Google was to my first book. I know there was a later set of articles around 1994 about rapes in Atlanta, but I can no longer find them. I tried going through my files a few years ago, but it was too painful. I need to let go of this trail. What I need is no longer "more confirmation"—I know my story. What I am trying to do is continue my life.

The blood-red bricks of my old house are gone. They have been covered over tastefully. And I find the gray comforting, elegant, calming. It is not as if one does not know that this house is made of brick; it is just different. Traces of what once was stand just next door. That large rambling structure is coming apart. It was sagging even then, but these days that house and yard bear the ravages of time, crumbling, neglected. I ran to the back door of that house to escape my attacker, and so I feel some abiding tenderness toward it. I had fantasized, that night, that the old southern man, the paterfamilias of the house, might run out with his shotgun and get the rapist, but even then he was frail, still looming but no longer vital. The couple next door helped me as I struggled to get through to 911. I suspect that the house was a bequest to this couple's daughter, a woman about ten years older than I am. I am not sure she was well then and I suspect that the house is in limbo, that she has not been able to attend to it, nor has she been able to sell it. This makes me sad. It is a reminder that things can play out so differently, thwarting our expectations and desires. The two houses are a study in contrasts, in the ravages of time, and in the healing power of money, investment, and renovation.

Svetlana Boym wrote that the inability to return home is both a personal tragedy and an enabling force. These two houses capture this paradox. Both renewal and decay are possible. And although I have been lucky, things might have been different. Returning to these two houses, to that time and this place, I am humbled by how much has changed.

Right now, I am hopeful. I see myself reflected in my former home. Although we are both older and grayer, we both stand tall. Like the ship *Argo*, we are still who and what we once were, even with all of these changes. And yet I need to say this once again: our stories could have been otherwise. There are no guarantees. We too might have ended up like the house next door, which just might also, over time, become something else.

I completed this book during the fall of 2018, not an easy season for those of us who live under the shadow of sexual violence. The rawness of recent public discourse has been painful. While writing, my greatest social contact has often come through Facebook. I guardedly post there, keeping afloat a range of relationships from very different parts of my life, folks who inhabit often conflicting worldviews. And although I have written at length about my rape over these many years, I am careful not to call too much attention to myself here.

The radical shift marked by the 2016 election has opened up my wound in a different way. Although I knew before, long before the Women's March, that I have an aversion to protests, these past few years, filled with so many friends and allies out on the streets, making calls, creating new advocacy organizations, doing such powerful work for the most vulnerable among us, I have stumbled, unable to fully engage in these efforts. I have felt myself torn. My admiration especially for my younger colleagues and friends who are doing this political work is immense, but my own reluctance to take part in those crowds has also grown more acute. And it is only in the past few weeks of writing this book that I finally came to appreciate why I cannot be a part of their number. On October 4, 2018, I wrote the following post on Facebook: "I am so not surprised by the news already . . . many of those of us who live with vivid memories of terrible things, have, I am afraid, learned to expect the worst time and time again. It is hard to feel hopeful. Part of what was taken away from me is outrage, political outrage. Outrage is fueled by a kind of hope that I no longer have."

Part of what rape took away from me was this kind of hope, something that was once quite familiar and ordinary. This kind of politics was a part of how I grew up. There is a double exposure, a snapshot taken at a teachers' strike in Dover, Delaware, dated August 1971. I was eleven. I am at the center of this image, holding a protest sign that reads in my own handwriting, "Save our Schools." Superimposed across my chest is a banner that reads "Capital Education Association"—the name of the teachers' union that my mother belonged to. She is also in this image, hardly visible, a small figure near my left shoulder, a strange angel looking out through a striking pair of sunglasses. I love this picture and I was happy to have found it after my mother's death. I have even posted it on Facebook. It sits on my computer desktop, and as I began writing these words it called out to me. She is the girl I once was, a protester carrying my own sign, on the street fighting for justice alongside her mother. That little girl is the person I lost, another casualty of rape. To be able to make those signs and join those crowds takes a kind of fortitude I no longer possess.

There were many responses to my Facebook post, loving and knowing. But there were also a few that were startled by what I had written, and it was hard for me not to feel compelled to protect them. I did not want to take away their hope. I just needed to be able to say that we don't all have this faith. This feeling is neither normal nor natural but rather a product of that fierce and profoundly hopeful outrage that I have lost and that I wish was still within my grasp. I miss it. And I am also aware of how much of what I wrote echoes not only my own adolescent mantra that it is best to think the worst, but also the kind of anxious prophylactic dread that Maggie Nelson shares with her mother.

A week later, the worst had already happened. I got a long private message triggered by current events but also by something in my post. The writer, with whom I share many friends and colleagues and who is someone I have come to know through the magic of Facebook, wrote in the hope that I might understand. My friend acknowledged that in some of my comments on Facebook I have alluded to something about my own experience that made the present moment difficult, triggering. She went on to explain that she was having a similar problem. She then told me a great deal about her struggles—painful, searing experiences that were now oozing out from under the shimmering veneer of her "great" life in the present. The terror in her life, something always close to the surface, was once again an opened wound demanding attention.

I write about these things so that others might not be alone. I know what that feels like. This is the kind of interaction that reminds me time and time again why sharing our stories matters. I eventually spoke to this friend over the phone. But first I wrote back, offering a brief version of my story. Despite being public about my rape, such intimacy always requires a retelling. This time, I wrote that I was raped in graduate school—my friend is also an academic—and I explained that the rapist was a stranger who broke into my home and threatened to kill me. I also explained that mine was a sadly familiar story and that it was now a cold case, more than twenty-five years old. I said that I had written about these things in the past and that I was also writing about them now. I explained that it is always hard. And then I wrote, perhaps even more directly, that it has been the loss of this political hope, this new acute ache, that I feel most keenly these days.

When my friend wrote back, she expressed her sadness about the fact that I was "brutally raped" and that the rapist threatened to kill me. Her language was more direct than my own, and I suppose that it was that direct statement of what had happened to me that shook me. In her voice, even on my screen, I heard my story differently. At first, I was afraid that I might have overstated what had happened to me. I scrambled in my head to undercut what she had said. It couldn't have been that bad. I woke up in the middle of the night thinking about this. Was what happened to me that bad? And I had to patiently let myself take all of this in. Isn't this what I have been saying for all these years? Isn't this what this book is all about? How do we live with knowing that the worst things can happen and have already happened?

But this time, I think there was something else that made this reckoning that much more startling. This time, being reminded by another that my life could have ended came with a deeper and more intimate knowledge of death and its finality. I took in this intimate and political moment. It was so unlike the time in 1992, after Anita Hill's testimony at Clarence Thomas's Supreme Court confirmation hearings, when my mother, after asking my permission, discussed my rape with Senator Joe Biden. He was trying to begin to make some kind of amends for his behavior at that hearing through the Violence Against Women Act (1994) that he would cosponsor. This time, I listened to this other woman's testimony, without my mother acting behind the scenes on my behalf. These many years later, I was alone. I had only my mother's ghostly presence in that photograph, a memento.

Over the past few months, I have found myself dreaming again. I no longer dream about lost dogs, though those dreams remain deeply familiar. The new recurring dream seems to be about crossings. I am on a bridge, already in motion, already on a journey trying to get to another place, but the way is not clear. The path ahead of me is treacherous. I am trying to get across a waterway, and there are huge waves. I may have to swim to make my way to the other side. In an early version of this new dream I got caught in the water and woke up afraid. But in the most recent of these dreams, I get out of my vehicle and begin walking, and despite the waves and currents, I move forward. There is a clearing. I make it to the other side. But I wake up before I can figure out where I am.

In my waking life, I also do not know exactly where I am heading. What I do know is that this work is carrying me to a different place. I am unsure about what comes next. But in the meantime, wherever I find myself, I hope that my words might reach at least a few readers who need them, that they offer the kind of embrace I found in Nelson's and de Waal's texts.

And perhaps in this writing and these dreams, I am beginning to appreciate more fully the power of new buildings and new containers as they bolster and stand alongside so many older structures that are being reconstituted.

New and renewed buildings and containers and the promise of the archive—all of these nested objects can and do remain vital as we continue to care for them. Not unlike relics and their reliquaries, their power is generative. It proliferates. The archival materials that Robert Jan van Pelt presented in court became the basis of *The Evidence Room*, allowing new generations to consider the legacy of the Holocaust, its architecture of destruction and the work of historians in telling its story. Not unlike that evidence, we too make and remake ourselves over time, figuring out again and again what we need to hold on to more or less tightly, and what we can let go. This is how we continue to inhabit our afterlives.

Notes

Introduction

1. See Levitt, *American Jewish Loss*.

2. Nelson, *Red Parts*, 118.

3. Although relics are most often associated with Catholic and Orthodox Christian traditions and were disparaged and rejected by Protestants, I am using the broader category of "Christian" in order to echo the language of the photographer Miki Kratsman, who deploys this discourse in his contemporary work. As historian Robert Wisniewski explains, "It was present in all currents of Christianity until the early modern period, when the rejection of the cult of relics became a distinguishing feature of the Reformed Churches." *Beginnings of the Cult of Relics*, 1. As I make clear in later chapters, in Europe and North America, engagement with relics is most often associated with Catholicism. For an interesting view of the afterlives of relics despite their disparagement, see Moshenska, *Iconoclasm as Child's Play*. For an account of Protestant fascination with Catholic objects, especially in miniature, see Franchot, "Unseemly Commemoration." On Orthodox engagements with relics, see Limberis, *Architects of Piety*.

4. See Peabody Museum of Archaeology and Ethnology at Harvard University, "Miki Kratsman: Gardner Photography Fellow, 2011," https://www.peabody.harvard.edu/node/692. See also Levitt, "Miki Kratsman."

5. Kratsman, *Resolution of the Suspect*, 151.

6. Bagnoli et al., *Treasures of Heaven*; Clifton, "Conversations in Museums"; Hahn, *Reliquary Effect*.

7. Unlike Emily Winslow, who was able to get her 1992 rape kit processed belatedly in 2013, I was never able to do this. See Winslow, "Saga of My Rape Kit."

8. Nelson, *Jane: A Murder*, 115, 116.

9. Ibid., 18.

10. I am increasingly confused about what, if any, objects the police took from my house. The official file records no inventory. There are other mistakes. But I was shocked to learn from Janet—during a phone conversation in June 2016, twenty-seven years after the rape—that on the night of my rape, the police who spoke to us in the hospital examining room explained that this was a neighborhood crime. As such, they said, the best way to catch the rapist would be for me to identify him on the street. I did not remember this conversation. I thought my vigilance came from elsewhere, from another graduate student who had been raped the year before I arrived. She had identified her rapist after seeing him on the street, and the case did go to court. Her story only reinforced what the police told us that night, according to Janet.

11. Nelson, *Jane: A Murder*, 23–25. This section begins with two poems titled "Figment."

12. I thank Susan E. Shapiro for helping formulate this account of my method and for her abiding critical engagement.

Chapter 1

1. The talk I heard was an early version of Biddick, "Arthur's Two Bodies." Biddick has since published this essay in *Make and Let Die*, 57–80.

2. Biddick, "Arthur's Two Bodies," 126. Shavuot is the Jewish celebration of "first fruits that commemorates the giving of the Torah." Biddick builds on Yuval, *Two Nations in Your Womb.*

3. Biddick, "Arthur's Two Bodies," 126.

4. Ibid.

5. Ibid., 127.

6. Yuval, *Two Nations in Your Womb,* 93–94, citing Rabbi Meir ben Shimon of Narbonne, *Milhemet Mitzvah* (The Commanding War). Yuval's work is hereafter cited parenthetically in the text.

7. As Yuval explains, "this metaphor of the crimson divine garment" also appears in a midrash cited in the medieval collection *Yalqut Shim'oni.* This midrash, which offers an extended discussion of this vision of messianic justice bound to the evidence collected in an archive of pain, reads, "Our Rabbis said: For every single soul of Israel that Esau killed, the Holy One blessed be He took from their blood and dipped in it His *porphyrion* until it was the color of blood; and when the Day of Judgment comes and He sits upon his dais to judge him [Esau], He will wear that *porphyrion* and show him the body of every righteous person that is recorded on it, as it is said, 'He will execute judgment among the nations, filling them with corpses.' At that selfsame time, the Holy One blessed be He executes against him a double vengeance as Scripture says, 'O Lord, thou God of vengeance, thou God of vengeance, shine forth!' [Ps. 94:1]." Ibid., 95.

8. According to *Black's Law Dictionary,* the term refers to "the body (material substance) upon which a crime has been committed, e.g.,

the corpse of a murdered man, the charred remains of a house burned down," but it also refers, "in a derivative sense, [to] the substance or foundation of a crime; the substantial fact that a crime has been committed." See "Corpus Delicti," http://thelawdictionary.org/corpus -delicti. In the secondary, derivative sense, the term is "also used to describe the evidence that proves a crime was committed"; see "Corpus Delicti," Free Dictionary, http://legal-dictionary .thefreedictionary.com/Corpus+delicti.

9. "Corpus Delicti," Free Dictionary, http:// legal-dictionary.thefreedictionary.com/Corpus +delicti.

10. As I aim to show later in this chapter, these two senses of corpus delicti blur the distinction between first- and second-order relics. For more on relics, see Brown, *Cult of the Saints.* I thank Leonard Primiano, Lisa Ratmansky, and Ava Chamberlain for suggesting that I consider this text and the larger question of Christian relics, during "The Creole Imagination Revisited: Anniversary Conference," Chateau d'Aragon, Aragon, France, June 13–20, 2015.

11. See Oldenhage, *Parables for Our Time* and *Neutestamentliche Passionsgeschichten.*

12. This vision of vengeance as deliverance sets up the account of the martyred Jews of Mainz, who are slaughtered by the crusaders there. The poem Biddick refers to in her brief account of this bloodied archival document, as Yuval explains, uses the word *vengeance* (*neqama*) fifteen times, along with the synonyms *gemul* (retribution), *tashlum* (payment), and the verbs *to wipe out* (*lekhalot*) and *to destroy* (*lehazmit*). Yuval, *Two Nations in Your Womb,* 105.

13. See Ezrahi, *Booking Passage.* On revenge fantasies and their dangers, see also Levitt, "Revenge: 2002." In a different way, the concept of revenge fantasies is vividly depicted in David Blumenthal's provocative reading of the Psalms in *Facing the Abusing God,* esp. chaps. 7–10 (67–192).

14. Ezrahi, *Booking Passage,* 21.

15. In making her case, Ezrahi too reminds us of the power of holding and, in the case of homecoming, its relation to death. As she explains, it is one thing to sojourn in the land, to live there without possessing it; but, following Arnold Eisen, she reminds us that in order to die in the land, "one needs a holding. So, when Sarah dies, Abraham must negotiate the purchase of a grave property." This, for Ezrahi, ties together her themes. "Exile and narrative, the time or *durée* of life itself, can yield only to homecoming, closure, and the place of (the place that is) death." Ibid., 21–22.

16. The vengeful Psalms offer a kind of homeopathic cure for painful communal ailments through more violence. To me, the reciting of such sacred texts—reading them alone or, perhaps more powerfully, as a communal act—might offer a way of coping more fully with communal harms. These texts might teach us something about what it means to live with terrible pain—with the sense of disappointment and betrayal, with the real harm that has not been made right and may never be redressed. Reading Blumenthal, I also worry about the dangers involved in reveling in such expressions of rage. For me, the Psalms were never supposed to be read literally. They were not meant to be reenacted. Rather, they were a way for us to acknowledge our pain and hurt within the context of a liturgical setting. This is partly why I find Ezrahi's approach so compelling.

17. Biddick, "Arthur's Two Bodies," 126.

18. Biddick, *Make and Let Die*, 24–25.

19. Ibid., 25, 26.

20. Nelson, *Red Parts*, 119.

21. See Ariella Azoulay, "From the Section 'The Natural History of Rape,' 'Enough! The Natural Violence of the New World Order,' F/ Stop Festival, Leipzig," Facebook, June 25, 2016, https://www.facebook.com/ariella .azoulay.5/posts/1022607011149413. See also Brown University, Pembroke Center for Teaching and Research on Women, "International Conference on Rape and War," April 15–16, 2016, https://www.brown.edu /research/pembroke-center/news/2016-04 /international-conference-rape-and-war.

22. Nelson writes eloquently in *The Red Parts* about her involvement in a protest against a death penalty case in Connecticut as her aunt's criminal case was unfolding. See "Murder Mind Redux," in *Red Parts*, 75–80.

Chapter 2

1. Levitt, "Speaking Out of the Silence," 21.

2. Subsequent editions of Nelson's memoir appeared with a different subtitle: *Autobiography of a Trial*.

3. Nelson's use of the phrase "the red parts" comes from red-letter editions of the Protestant Bible, which print the words of Jesus in red. But the practice of printing in red has a longer Christian history, including the "rubrication" of instructions in a printed Christian liturgy; "rubrication" means printing in red. From this practice, the term "rubric" acquired the secondary connotation of printed nonreligious instructions—for example, in legal documents in which a title, heading, or section is printed in red. Nelson's account of the legal trial of her aunt's murderer carries these resonances, even as she undermines their authority. The first red-letter Bible was printed in 1899 by a man named Louis Klopsch. Legend has it that Klopsch was inspired by Luke 22:20, "This cup is the new testament in my blood, which I shed for you": a red part. Here, the blood of Jesus is merged with his words, shed and shared for those who believe. For more on the history of red-letter Bibles, see Crossway, "The Origins of the Red-Letter Bible," March 23, 2006, https://www.crossway .org/blog/2006/03/red-letter-origin; Steve Eng, "Story Behind: Red Letter Bible Editions," *Bible Collectors' World*, January–March 1986, http:// www.biblecollectors.org/articles/red_letter _bible.htm.

4. I thank Dawn Skorczewski for this insight. The term "choiceless choice" comes from Lawrence Langer. As he explains, choiceless choices are "crucial decisions [that]

did not reflect options between life and death, but between one form of abnormal response and another." "Dilemma of Choice in the Deathcamps," 57.

5. "*Whosoever shall seek to save his life shall lose it; and whosoever shall lose his life shall preserve it.* Another red part." Nelson, *Red Parts*, 88, quoting Luke 17:33.

6. Levitt, *Jews and Feminism*, 23 (hereafter cited parenthetically in the text).

7. Nelson, *Red Parts*, 89.

8. Ibid., 90.

9. Ibid., 79.

10. This is another iteration of Luke 17:33.

11. Levitt, "Revisiting the Property Room."

12. Winnicott, "Psychology of Madness," 126. For more on this dynamic, see Winnicott, "Fear of Breakdown."

13. Nelson, *Red Parts*, 151.

14. Yasco Horsman addresses this question in a different context in *Theaters of Justice.* But in that book, justice is ultimately about what we owe the dead, especially after the Holocaust. I prefer Nelson and Voltaire on the issue, or Irena Klepfisz, who dedicates her narrative poem "*Bashert*" to both those who died and those who survived. I am interested in this double obligation to both the living and the dead.

15. Nelson, *Red Parts*, 88.

Chapter 3

1. "Years before," Maggie Nelson writes, "I had had a lover who was a welder. As a gift he once welded me the single most beautiful object that I own. It is a palm-sized box made of Plexiglas, with several stacked layers of blue-greenish broken glass sealed inside. The box, he explained to me, is the love. It is the container that can hold all of the brokenness, and make it beautiful. Especially when you hold it up to the light." Nelson, *Red Parts*, 85.

2. De Waal, *Hare with Amber Eyes,* 17 (hereafter cited parenthetically in the text).

3. I quote the translation in Berlin and Brettler, *Jewish Study Bible*, 963. Unless otherwise noted, all translations of Jeremiah

are from this text. A different translation uses slightly different language; the vessel was "marred," suggesting a less moralizing account of this imperfection: "And whensoever the vessel that he made of the clay was marred in the hand of the potter, he made it again another vessel, as seemed good to the potter to make it." Early Jewish Writings, "Jeremiah."

4. See Berlin and Brettler's note on these verses (18:1–23), *Jewish Study Bible*, 963.

5. Playing with the connection between two related but different meanings of the term *yotzer, devising* and *potter* (*Jewish Study Bible*, 963, note for verses 18:11–17), some translations bring back the figure of the potter here. See, for example, the translation of 18:11 in the New Revised Standard Version: "Look, I am a potter shaping evil against you and devising a plan against you. Turn now, all of you from your evil ways, and amend your ways and your doings."

6. *The Jewish Study Bible* connects this feminized rhetoric to tropes and figures found in wisdom literature; in a note to verses 18:13–15, the editors describe "*Maiden Israel*" as God's metaphorical "wife." They go on to explain that "a series of accusations then follows in which God claims to have been abandoned by Israel." Berlin and Brettler, *Jewish Study Bible*, 963–64.

7. See Magid, "Jewish Renewal and the Holocaust."

8. Sara Ahmed, keynote address, National Women's Studies Association Annual Meeting, Milwaukee, Wisconsin, November 13, 2015; Ahmed, "Feminism and Fragility." See especially "Fragile Things," section 1 of the latter. Ahmed writes about objects breaking in two George Eliot novels; in this case, the focus is on brokenness but the objects broken are all made of clay; they are useful everyday vessels whose brokenness provides not only an opening for narrative but a loss of quotidian intimacy. In the first example, from *Silas Marner*, Ahmed writes, "Silas is touched by his pot. The pot is his companion; reliable; always in the same spot, always lending its handle." She describes

this "relationship of use" as one of affection, of "shared history." And when it breaks, it loses its usefulness and becomes a memorial. This form of tender engagement captures well the affective relationship between objects and their holders.

9. Vitrines are an abiding part of de Waal's own artistic work and figure prominently in many of his most recent exhibitions. See, for example, the account of a piece shown in an exhibition that opened in Venice in the spring of 2019, in Harris, "Edmund de Waal to Create Exhibition."

10. In the fall of 2018, it seems that the collection changed hands. Not only did Edmund de Waal and his family decide to auction seventy-nine of the netsukes to raise funds for refugees, but Edmund decided to place the rest of the collection on long-term loan to the Jewish Museum in Vienna. See Luke, "'Total Crisis in Europe'"; and Harris, "Edmund de Waal's Famed Netsuke Collection." The netsukes return to Vienna as a testament to their own diasporic existence, in the hope that they might speak to the lives of others who have been displaced and made vulnerable in the present historical moment. As Gareth Harris writes, "De Waal has specified that the netsuke can be handled by the public at the Jewish Museum in Vienna. An exhibition based on the family collection, which will also tour internationally, is due to open late next year." Not only this, but in a statement Harris quotes, de Waal explained, "The decision to place the netsuke on loan allows them to tell the story of migration, identity and exile to a new audience. In *The Hare with Amber Eyes*, I wrote of how objects can evoke histories through touch, and a stipulation of the loan is that a group will be available for handling by the many visitors to the [Jewish] Museum." De Waal donated his family archive to the museum as well.

11. De Waal writes about his fascination with porcelain and its history in *White Road*.

12. Shallcross, *Holocaust Object*, 6.

13. Hair is especially challenging. Great controversy surrounded its inclusion in the permanent exhibit at the USHMM. And even when the curators decided not to display the actual hair (on loan to the museum from Auschwitz), inclusion of the photograph of those bales of hair was still controversial. For more on this hair, see chap. 5, "The Arts of Conservation and Collections Management." Hair also holds the promise of the DNA that Nelson writes about. I thank Ruth Ost for reminding me of these intense resonances.

14. As Shallcross argues in the conclusion of her book, all we have inherited are "shreds." And this: "One observation is unequivocal: the post-Holocaust material world is the domain of both traces and vestiges entrusted to us to read them and grant continuation." *Holocaust Object*, 136.

15. The lush figure of the tears of things is also the subject and the title of a beautiful literary study about our attachments to objects. See Schwenger, *Tears of Things*.

Chapter 4

1. For more on these issues, see Biber, "Cultural Afterlife of Criminal Evidence."

2. This definition comes from "IAPE Professional Standards and Document," *IAPE*, http://home.iape.org/evidence-resources/iape-documents.html.

3. See, for example, the ongoing work of the Joyful Heart Foundation and the Rape, Abuse, and Incest National Network (RAINN). See also Rape Kit Action Project, https://everykitcounts.org; and "About RAINN," https://www.rainn.org/about-rainn.

4. See FBI, "Combined DNA Index System (CODIS)," https://www.fbi.gov/services/laboratory/biometric-analysis/codis.

5. See Yerebakan, "Making Installations Out of Rape Kits." My thanks to Aliza Shvarts for thinking with me about these issues, and to Ann Pellegrini for introducing us.

6. For example, the tragic case of gross negligence in which custody was granted to the biological parents of a young boy, Khalil Wimes, whose interests were failed by the courts and the child protective services. Khalil died of

malnutrition and gross neglect at the age of six. See "Khalil Wimes' Foster Family," WHYY, https://whyy.org/episodes/a-conversation-with-the-foster-family-of-khalil-wimes-2.

7. As I read various definitions of custody, I was reminded of how objects are made into evidence. Objects become evidence when the law beckons them, and this process is performative. Judith Butler's notion of the subject constituted by the law, including her broader notion of identity as performative, echoes much of what I am saying here. See Butler, *Gender Trouble*, 5 (esp. nn. 1 and 2), 192.

8. See Rush, *Dictionary of Criminal Justice*, 45.The definition given here is the same as that given in Latta and Rush, *Evidence and Property Management,* v.

9. This concept is very much in keeping with the kind of careful accounting that art conservators do as they record in detail their work with the objects in their care. My thanks to art conservator Liz Peirce for explaining these practices to me.

10. Again, this form of documentation is standard practice in the work of art conservation, as we shall see, and I am again indebted to Liz Peirce for teaching me about this process.

11. Fordham University, Graduate School of Social Service, "MSW Process Recording Handbook," https://www.fordham.edu/downloads/file/3680/msw_process_recording_handbook.

12. As Latta and Rush note, there are many titles for such professionals, among them property manager, property controller, evidence controller, evidence technician, and property custodian. Latta and Rush, *Evidence and Property Management*, xi.

13. Ibid.

14. More up-to-date versions of some of these texts, and more recent accounts of evidence law, include *The Federal Rules of Evidence: 2018 Edition*; Beitman, *Getting Your Hands on the Evidence*; Friedman, *Elements of Evidence*; American Law Institute, *Model Code*

of Evidence; Wigmore, *Treatise on the System of Evidence*; Halsted, *Halsted's Digest of the Law of Evidence*; and Hanley and Schmidt, *Introduction to Criminal Evidence.*

15. The notion that evidence cannot speak for itself is echoed resoundingly in recent critical work on forensics. See, for example, Keenan and Weizman, *Mengele's Skull.*

16. Scott, "Women's History," 241.

17. Ibid.

18. Ibid, 243.

19. Scholars of photography and film recognize how we handle, hold in our hands, and at the same time capture the haptic qualities of both photographic and cinematic film in notions of haptic visuality (Laura Marks) and haptic photographic practices (Margaret Olin). See Marks, *Skin of Film*; Olin, *Touching Photographs*; Olin, "About Touching Photographs," https://touchingphotographs.com/about.

20. Latta and Rush, *Evidence and Property Management*, 1.

21. As Latta and Rush explain, "Some law enforcement agencies are reluctant to use non-sworn personnel in the property room due to their being 'trustworthy.' A recent review of approximately 300 newspaper articles showed the opposite to be true. These accounts revealed that nearly 80 percent of employees who were disciplined, indicted, imprisoned or killed were sworn officers!" Ibid., 5.

22. Latta, *Property and Evidence by the Book*, chap. 2, 2 (each chapter's pagination begins with 1).

23. Ibid., 2, 2–3.

24. Ratcliff, "Confronting Evidence," 201.

25. Kennedy, "Larry Sultan, California Photographer."

26. "Sultan and Mandel: 'Evidence–Larry Sultan and Mike Mandel' (1977)," American Suburb X, October 19, 2009, http://www.americansuburbx.com/2009/10/theory-evidence-larry-sultan-and-mike.html.

27. See the BAM/PFA interview with Mike Mandel, Larry Sultan, and Jim Goldberg, with

Constance Lewallen, https://www.youtube.com/watch?v=9GSm-P1zJps&spfreload=1.

28. Ibid.

29. "Sultan and Mandel," American Suburb X.

30. Derrida, *Truth in Painting*, 332.

31. I wrote about this in "Revisiting the Property Room"; see esp. n. 17.

32. Ratcliff, "Confronting Evidence," 202.

33. Boscagli, *Stuff Theory*, 202.

34. Woolf, *To the Lighthouse*, 129; see also Boscagli, *Stuff Theory,* 204.

35. Boscagli, *Stuff Theory*, 204–5. The quotations in the following two paragraphs are also from *Stuff Theory*, 205. (Boscagli misspells Ramsay "Ramsey"; I have corrected this error silently.)

Chapter 5

1. Kristine Keren changed her name when she came to the United States. She published her story, *The Girl in the Green Sweater: A Life in Holocaust's Shadow,* under her given name, Krystyna Chiger. For more on this sweater and its story, see also USHMM, "A Cherished Object: Kristine Keren's Green Sweater," https://www.ushmm.org/collections /the-museums-collections/curators-corner /a-cherished-object-kristine-kerens-green -sweater; and the 2011 film *In Darkness, directed by* Agnieszka Holland.

2. Nelson, *Red Parts*, 184.

3. On the logic of analogy, see Jakobsen, "Queers Are Like Jews." I offer a sustained account of the challenge of analogy in Levitt, "Rescued Evidence."

4. Foer, *Everything Is Illuminated*, 147. The following quotations are also from p. 147.

5. On Komar and Melamid's "People's Choice" project, see Wypijewski, *Painting by Numbers*. Conservation as a practice echoes quite directly this tension as both an art and a science. For a beautiful account of the practices of art and science, see Ward, *Nature of Conservation*. My thanks to Liz Peirce for this reference and for her insights into the labors of conservation.

6. Boym, *Another Freedom*, 285–86. The quotations in the following two paragraphs are from ibid., 286–89.

7. These thoughts were inspired by conversations with Ruth Ost and her artworks; see Ost's cover image in Levitt, "Changing Focus."

8. Williams and Tsien, *Wunderkammer*.

9. Conservation and preservation are distinct though interrelated endeavors. I have tried to stay close to my sources in my discussion of these matters. I thank Jane Klinger, chief conservator at the USHMM, for calling my attention to the difference between the two practices.

10. For an account of this image and the story of these children and their family, see USHMM, "From Image to Rescue: The Gavra Mandil Collection," https://www.ushmm.org /collections/the-museums-collections/curators -corner/from-image-to-rescue-the-gavra-mandil -collection.

11. See http://www.ushmm.org/information /press/press-releases/united-states-holocaust -memorial-museum-and-banca-civica-cooperate -to-rescu.

12. The Jack, Joseph and Morton Mandel Center for Advanced Holocaust Studies is a crucial component of the USHMM's mission. Although scholars have focused primarily on the permanent collection, I am interested in the institution's role as a research center, archive, and library. The exhibition and the research center share a commitment to amassing evidence. See USHMM, "About the Mandel Center."

13. According to *Merriam-Webster's*, the curate's role was as "a member of the clergy in certain churches (such as the Anglican church) who assists the priest in charge of a church or a group of churches," but Wikipedia explains that a curate "is a person who is invested with the *care* or *cure (cura) of souls* of a parish. In this sense 'curate' correctly means a parish priest; but in English-speaking countries the

term *curate* is commonly used to describe clergy who are assistants to the parish priest. The duties or office of a curate are called a curacy (as the office of a president is a presidency)." I am struck by the caring role of the curate who watches over his congregation, a collection of souls whose symptoms must be attended to. And it is strange how this role becomes the domain of the priest's assistants, his supplements, who, especially as the plural suggests, have a great deal of work to do, requiring many hands. Such caretaking is quite labor intensive.

14. Ward, *Nature of Conservation*, 1.

15. On the question of excess, see Hansen-Glucklich, *Holocaust Memory Reframed*, chap. 5, "'We Are the Last Witnesses': Artifacts, Aura, and Authenticity."

16. In the discussion that follows, I build on insights gleaned from three works by Oren Stier—"Torah and Taboo"; *Holocaust Icons*; and *Committed to Memory*—and Hansen-Glucklich, *Holocaust Memory Reframed*. Although many excellent works address the history of the USHMM, I focus on these works because of their attention to the material evidence at the heart of the collection and its display. Avril Alba considers the sacred quality of Holocaust museums, but her work focuses less on the animate quality of sacred objects than on their narrative implications. In her book *Holocaust Memorial Museum,* Alba offers a Jewish theological reading of the display of objects, and she notes the difference between her approach and those of Stier and Hansen-Glucklich. This study, like those works, addresses the visual and material cultures of religion rather than explicitly Jewish theology as metahistory or Holocaust museums as redemptive. For a reading of Jewish ritual and Holocaust commemoration that resists Alba's kind of redemptive reading, see Gubkin, *You Shall Tell Your Children.*

17. Hansen-Glucklich, *Holocaust Memory Reframed*, 121, 129, 127. As Hansen-Glucklich observes, the logic of this museum shares many of the display techniques common to the museums on the sites of concentration camps, where authentic objects are central. James Young also notes that amassing and displaying lots of material evidence at the USHMM was intended to challenge the claims of Holocaust deniers: "Though director Jeshajahu Weinberg believes such artifacts make the factuality of the Holocaust self-evident, an immunization against the negationist lies that deny the Holocaust, they also suggest something the Holocaust was not: a collection of ownerless items, junked." Young adds that when "an entire people is represented by the artifacts of their lives, something of life itself is lost." Young, *Texture of Memory*, 346.

18. Hansen-Glucklich, *Holocaust Memory Reframed*, 128.

19. On the Museum of Tolerance and the logic of its display, see Derwin, "Sense and/or Sensation"; and Stier, "Virtual Memories." Stier expands this argument in *Committed to Memory*, chap. 4, "Mediating Memory: Holocaust Museums and the Display of Remembrance."

20. See Stier, *Holocaust Icons*, esp. chap. 3, "Different Trains: Holocaust Artifacts and the Ideologies of Remembrance."

21. Crew and Sims, "Locating Authenticity."

22. Hansen-Glucklich echoes Thomas Laqueur's critique of the museum here: "In Washington, a plenum claims to speak for loss." Quoted in *Holocaust Memory Reframed*, 135.

23. "One might argue, as does Linenthal, that these artifacts are 'domesticated' and rendered 'safer to view' due to such displacement." Ibid., 132. See also Stier, *Committed to Memory*, 110–49.

24. Liliane Weissberg suggests that "the United States Holocaust Memorial Museum, bearing a national claim in its very name, does not only delimit the effort of journeying, but also that of having to consider another country, Israel, as a safe harbor for Jews." "Memory Confined," 54. I am grateful to Oren Stier for directing me to this essay; see Stier, "Torah and Taboo," 510.

25. On the choice of Washington as the location for the museum, see Weissberg, "Memory Confined," 67–73.

26. I am grateful to art historians Barbara Mundy and Gabriella Costa for helping me appreciate these works more fully. They helped me see the irony in securing one's place in the windows of a cathedral that was bombed, necessitating the windows' replacement. This abiding longing for permanence continues to inform my thinking.

27. I am also reminded of the enthusiasm expressed by so many survivors who told their stories to Steven Spielberg for what became the USC Shoah Foundation. The archive began in 1994, after Spielberg had completed his Oscar-winning film *Schindler's List*. The allure of the project lay in its name brand, the stature of the filmmaker, and the financial resources that secured the collection. For the history of the USC Shoah Foundation and the Institute for Visual History and Education, see USC Shoah Foundation, "Institute History Timeline," https://sfi.usc.edu/about/history.

28. Weissberg, "Memory Confined," 56. For a different view of the USHMM's original use of identity cards, see Liss, *Trespassing Through Shadows*, esp. chap. 2, "The Identity Card Project and the Tower of Faces at the United States Holocaust Memorial Museum."

29. Weissberg, "Memory Confined," 56–58. See also Young, *Texture of Memory*, 344.

30. In many instances, it was not so much a passport but a visa that determined the difference between life and death. I thank the museum's chief conservator, Jane Klinger, for this clarification.

31. The USHMM thus performs what Ward describes as the four classic functions of all museums, though perhaps with a much heavier focus than most on the use of the collection for ongoing research. Ward, *Nature of Conservation*.

32. This has changed somewhat with the opening of the new state-of-the-art storage facility in Bowie, Maryland. See McNamara, "U.S. Holocaust Museum Research Center Opens."

33. The renaming took place on the occasion of the dedication of the Shapell Center. The online collections search catalogue, art and artifacts, photography, film, and audio collections, along with conservators, librarians, archivists, etc., are all a part of the NIHD. My thanks to Travis Roxlau, the director of Collections Services at the USHMM, for this clarification.

34. Its overarching database can now be accessed at USHMM, "Search Our Collections," http://collections.ushmm.org/search.

35. Stier, *Committed to Memory, 42* (hereafter cited parenthetically in the text).

36. Hair is complicated. Its display and circulation mark it as different from other human remains. Human hair can be sold, for example, while the sale of other human remains is prohibited (with an exception for human skeletons, which can be purchased for medical use). On such rules and prohibitions, see eBay's "Human Body Parts Policy," http://pages.ebay.com/help/policies/remains.html. I thank Leonard Primiano for alerting me to these issues and for sending me to the eBay site at a workshop titled "Creole Religious Imagination Revisited," held in Aragon, France, June 14, 2015.

37. Linenthal is quoted in Stier, *Committed to Memory*. Stier returns to these debates in much more detail in "Torah and Taboo," where he describes some of the halakhic issues raised by the display of human hair. Here, he draws more intimate connections between this sacred relic and the desecrated Torah scrolls also on display at the museum. Stier presents archival records from 1989 until about 1992 to describe some of the arguments about whether to request human hair as part of the permanent exhibition and the ongoing ethical challenges involved in its display. Stier, "Torah and Taboo," 522–30.

38. That is, the original storage facility. See Price, "U.S. Holocaust Memorial Museum."

39. My thanks to Jane Klinger, the museum's chief conservator, and Travis Roxlau, the director of Collections Services, for discussing this with me in August 2014. In fact, this entire section is indebted to my conversations with Klinger, Roxlau, and many other USHMM librarians, curators, conservators, and property managers during my visit in 2014.

40. Boyle, "Auschwitz-Birkenau Barracks."

41. "Inherent vice" is described in ways that echo the novel *Inherent Vice* by Thomas Pynchon.

42. Hansen-Glucklich, *Holocaust Memory Reframed*, 129.

43. This account comes from my conversations with Jane Klinger, August 4–15, 2014. It is by no means a definitive account. For more on the shoes and their display, see Hansen-Glucklich, *Holocaust Memory Reframed*, esp. 129–36.

44. National Archives, Archives Library Information Center, "Intrinsic Value in Archival Material," http://www.archives.gov/research /alic/reference/archives-resources/archival -material-intrinsic-value.html.

45. On these professional practices, see Merritt, *National Standards and Best Practices*. Along with careful guidance on how to manage a museum and address various ethical, legal, and safety concerns, section 4, "Collections Stewardship," is most interesting. Its guidelines clarify the USHMM's in terms of its various acquisition and loan policies, including the loan of shoes from Majdanek. Oddly enough, the policy guide has two sections—"Standards Regarding the Unlawful Appropriation of Objects During the Nazi Era" and "Best Practices Regarding the Unlawful Appropriation of Objects During the Nazi Era"—that do not actually apply to the work of the USHMM. They include specific guidelines for otherwise valuable properties, most especially artworks.

46. Klinger's own research is on such objects, both individual and communal, and builds on work on disaster research and questions of vulnerability. She was completing her dissertation in the conservation program at the University of Delaware when we met. See her "Objects of Trauma."

47. Conversation with librarian Vincent E. Slatt, USHMM, August 2014.

48. Hansen-Glucklich, *Holocaust Memory Reframed*, 129.

49. Quoted in ibid., 131.

50. Young, *Texture of Memory*, 127.

51. Young builds on French historian Pierre Nora's work on archives and collective memory. For a more radical critique of the idea of unmediated evidence, see Nichanian, *Historiographic Perversion*. Mediation is also unavoidable in the labor of forensics and the deployment of "forensic evidence," which can never speak for itself but must always be contextualized and explained. See Keenan and Weizman, *Mengele's Skull*. I am grateful to Stephenie Young for this reference and for her work on forensic photography, and for her role as co-convener of the USHMM summer workshop "Literary Responses to Genocide in the Post-Holocaust Era," Mandel Center for Advanced Holocaust Studies, August 4–15, 2014.

52. Young, *Texture of Memory*, 127.

53. Young continues, "The archivists' traditional veneration of the trace is tied directly to their need for proof and evidence of a particular past. But in this they too often confuse proof that something existed with proof that it existed in a particular way, for seemingly self-evident reasons." Ibid., 127. Nichanian offers a brutal critique of this confusion as it pertains to the discourse of perpetrators; he is especially skeptical about the logic of the archive and the labor of witnessing. See *Historiographic Perversion*, chap. 3, "Refutation," and chap. 4, "Testimony: From Document to Monument."

54. "Numinous," a term borrowed from the religious realm, is how Jane Klinger describes many visitors' reactions to the shoes. For more on Christian rites and rituals, see Wisniewski, *Beginnings of the Cult of Relics*, and Freeman, *Holy Bones, Holy Dust*. It is also noteworthy that Avril Alba describes the ritual of burying

ashes and human remains at various Holocaust museums as both a Jewish and a universal practice. She describes these efforts as akin to "the long-standing Christian practice of the 'incorporation of relics.'" Alba, *Holocaust Memorial Museum*, 36.

55. Hansen-Glucklich, *Holocaust Memory Reframed*, 133.

56. Auslander, "Beyond Words," 1016.

57. Hughes, "Mysterium Materiae," 16.

58. Hughes writes, "To date, religious studies has not crafted an interpretive language capable of encompassing these objects. The Protestant-normative, Reformationist, Western, and utterly 'American' ethos of religious studies—its preoccupation with belief over practice, with the invisible *mysterium* over the material *tremendum*, its reverence for the interior and disdain for the exterior—these have hindered the development of a theoretical apparatus capable of approximating and interpreting the complex role of living matter in diverse religious practices." Ibid.

59. Ibid., 17, 18. According to Hughes, the discourse of the new materialism in anthropology has had a similarly allergic reaction to religious language. Hughes cites a key work on this subject, Bennett, *Vibrant Matter*, on pp. 20–22. Hughes writes of "the consecrated host—arguably another manifestation of vital matter" (19), only to turn her attention to this new literature that should be more closely aligned with religious studies. She calls for ontological revisions, critiquing this trend in anthropological theory since 2000 that places vital objects at the center of scholarly analysis.

60. On a pair of red children's shoes, among other object stories from the USHMM collection, see "The Last Witnesses: Artifacts from the Museum's Collection," https://www.ushmm.org/information/about-the-museum/museum-publications/the-last-witnesses.

61. Weissberg, "Memory Confined," 62, 63.

62. On the power and allure of such objects, see Auslander, "Beyond Words."

63. Weissberg, "Memory Confined," 63.

64. USHMM, "Collections, Conservation and Research Center," https://www.ushmm.org/support/why-support/collections-and-conservation-center.

65. Jeffrey Shandler offers a compelling account of the power of objects in the memory of Holocaust survivors in the final chapter of *Holocaust Memory in the Digital Age*, 125–66.

66. USHMM, *Safeguarding Truth Forever*, https://www.ushmm.org/support/why-support/collections-and-conservation-center/safeguarding-truth-forever.

67. For more on the possibilities opened up by such online displays, see Levitt, "Revisiting the Property Room." For *Curators Corner*, see USHMM, "Curators Corner, Extraordinary Stories Behind the Objects in Our Collections," https://www.ushmm.org/collections/the-museums-collections/curators-corner.

Chapter 6

1. Nightingale, "'Broken Knowledge,'" 15. On wonder, see also Nightingale, "On Wandering and Wondering"; Kandiyoti, "Imagining Cosmopolitanism"; Landy and Saler, "Introduction"; and Rubenstein, *Strange Wonder*.

2. Laura Levitt, "From My Father's Visual Archive: A Lost American Jewish Home," presentation at the conference "No Direction Home: Re-imagining Jewish Geography," Lehigh University, Bethlehem, Pennsylvania, March 2007.

3. As I wrote long ago, "citations of other people's writing can brace our own argument, providing weight, authority, and precedent. But sometimes in this process, a writer gets lost. As readers who write about other people's writing, we can lose our own voices, holding on too tightly to the authority of other people's writing." Levitt, "(Problem with) Embraces," 215.

4. Eliade, *The Sacred and the Profane*, 11–12.

5. See Nagel, "Afterlife of the Reliquary."

6. Derrida writes of Van Gogh's painting *Old Shoes*, "The pair inhibits, at least, if it does

not prevent, the 'fetishizing' movement; it rivets things to use, to 'normal' use." Derrida, *Truth in Painting*, 332.

7. Hughes, "Cradling the Sacred."

8. See Levitt, "Rites and Rituals of Holding." And for a somewhat different take, see Levitt, "Ritual and Rites in Holocaust Commemoration."

9. This account echoes and also challenges James Young's critique of a later version of fetishization, a kind of Enlightenment version of this practice. Young makes a powerful argument for resisting any notion of "unmediated history," but he dismisses the affective power of these objects and perhaps some of the ways in which they may in fact "embody the spirit of the people who made and used them." *Texture of Memory*, 127. I want to risk fetishization—not so as to have unmediated access to these artifacts, but rather so as to appreciate how they cannot be contained by any law of normal usage.

10. Stallybrass and Jones, "Fetishizing the Glove," 174. For a somewhat different view, see Young, *Texture of Memory*. On Protestant iconoclasm, see Freeman, *Holy Bones, Holy Dust*, chap. 23, "Protestantism and the New Iconoclasm." For the ways in which these efforts create new forms of worship and play, see Moshenska, *Iconoclasm as Child's Play*.

11. Stallybrass and Jones, "Fetishizing the Glove," 175.

12. This is a crucial piece of Moshenska's central argument in *Iconoclasm as Child's Play*. Efforts to dispose of and disempower once sacred objects often lead to their reanimation.

13. Although there are many just criticisms of Novick's groundbreaking study *Holocaust in American Life*, I turn to it here not so much to address those criticisms but to call attention to what Novick takes for granted and how he repeats a set of convictions that echo the Protestant condemnation of Catholic material religion in order to show the specter of these assumptions, which are alive and well in American Holocaust commemoration. Novick's critique of the material aspects of Holocaust commemoration are critical to my larger argument.

14. For a strong critique of Novick's temporal claims about Holocaust consciousness, see Diner, *We Remember with Love*. For a different reading of Diner's text in relation to Jewish memory of the Holocaust, see Alba, *Holocaust Memorial Museum*, esp. 82–84. For a powerful reading of how and what the Holocaust, as an extreme case history, teaches us about historical understanding more generally, see also Confino, *Foundational Pasts*.

15. As I will further explain, Novick builds his case primarily around the material practices of religion, arguing for a modernist vision that has superseded such atavistic enactments. See Sally Promey's introduction and conclusion in Promey, *Sensational Religion*.

16. Novick, *Holocaust in American Life*, 10 (hereafter cited parenthetically in the text).

17. See my reference to this work in the introduction to this book and in Levitt, "Miki Kratsman."

18. Promey, *Sensational Religion*, 7, 4.

19. I also want to draw attention to another distinction that Novick glosses over, and that is the difference between what he disparages as "fetishized objects" and what he calls "symbolic representations." Refusing the allegorical and staying with the concrete is crucial. It allows these objects to help us remember in tangible terms specific losses, atrocities, and crimes. The objects are not symbols of anything else. They are what they are and as such are talismanic. This is Maggie Nelson's point.

20. See Eliade, *The Sacred and the Profane*.

21. Where and how do we mourn with so little? This is the tragedy of not being able to visit a grave, of not being able to do the rituals of mourning that are so critical to Jewish traditions of all kinds, secular and religious. This is, in part, what Yizkor Bikher memorial works are all about: struggles to find alternative forms of mourning. See Kugelmass and Boyarin, *From a Ruined Garden*; Friedman, "Reckoning with Ghosts."

22. Promey, *Sensational Religion*, 12. Echoing Promey in a different key, Joe Moshenska shows in *Iconoclasm as Child's Play* how even iconoclasm can become a new form of worship and reverence all over again.

23. Robert Jan van Pelt's *The Evidence Room* was his contribution to the 2016 Architecture Biennale in Venice. The title refers to both the exhibition and the companion book about the creation of this work; see Bordeleau et al., *Evidence Room*. On the Biennale, see the two-volume exhibition catalogue, *Reporting from the Front: Biennale Architecture 2016*.

24. Bordeleau et al., *Evidence Room*, 76 (hereafter cited parenthetically in the text).

25. As I was completing this book in early 2019, I learned that Edmund de Waal also planned to go to Venice to create his own reliquary space, another room filled with vitrines; see Harris, "Edmund de Waal to Create Exhibition." The photograph that accompanies Harris's article shows a white cube, a space not so different from that of *The Evidence Room*. It is also noteworthy that de Waal auctioned off some of his precious netsuke collection to raise money for the support of refugees, and announced his plan to place the rest of his netsuke collection on long-term loan to the Jewish Museum in Vienna. Writing about that decision, de Waal explained that he stipulated that visitors be able to touch the netsukes and hold them in their hands. Harris, "Edmund de Waal's Famed Netsuke Collection."

26. The exhibit is now in the care of the Evidence Room Foundation and made its US debut in the summer of 2019 at the Hirshhorn Museum in Washington, DC. The foundation is committed to seeing that *The Evidence Room* continues to circulate. For more on the foundation and its work, see https://evidenceroomfoundation.com. About this iteration of the exhibition, see Levitt, "Holocaust Memory."

27. See Young, "Geographies of Loss."

28. Nagel, "Afterlife of the Reliquary," 212.

29. I keep thinking about how *The Evidence Room* was critiqued for being perhaps too beautiful. It is, after all, a stark and striking forensic production. And yet, how else do we show respect and reverence? See, for example, Schuessler, "'Evidence Room.'" I am also reminded of the magnificent boxes at the USHMM designed to hold the extremely fragile wedding dresses made of nylon parachutes in displaced persons' camps just after the war. These hopeful repurposed garments, created by survivors in order to celebrate life after the horrors of the Holocaust, to ritually enact the promise of a future, of love and family, are themselves kept safe in those reliquaries.

30. Writing about this challenge, curator James Clifton explained that the Plexiglas cases at the British Museum performed "a doubling of the reliquaries in which they [the relics] are already housed." The vitrines, he said, in fact "augment the objects' special status and the viewers' longing to experience their sacred force, even in the context of a secular museum." "Conversations in Museums," 210. In addition, "visitors were free to touch, kiss, or otherwise engage in religious *frottage* with the relic-related gifts in the gift shop situated at the end of the exhibition"; this "may have provided an outlet for pent-up tactile yearnings" (210). On rubbing, see Iversen, *Photography, Trace, and Trauma*, esp. chap. 4, "Casting, Rubbing, Making Strange."

31. Nagel, "Afterlife of the Reliquary," 213.

32. Ibid., 212.

33. See Saieh, "Venice Biennale 2012"; Williams and Tsien, *Wunderkammer*.

34. This process is in the spirit of the ship *Argo,* which is rebuilt bit by bit over time even as it maintains its name. There is both continuity and change. The story of the *Argo* was the inspiration for Maggie Nelson's award-winning 2015 book *The Argonauts,* a book about love and its renewal as bodies change bit by bit. Reading *The Argonauts* helped me see these connections.

35. Nelson, *Red Parts,* 184 (hereafter cited parenthetically in the text).

36. In a late section of *The Argonauts*, Maggie Nelson describes a gift from her lover

early in their relationship that she describes as an "art-weapon," a "talisman of protection—a means of keeping myself safe while you were gone. . . . I've kept it by my bedside ever since. Not because I think they're coming for us per se. But because it makes the brutal tender" (118). Rather than a traditional weapon used in combat, this artistic creation offered a kind of magical protection.

Bibliography

Ahmed, Sara. "Feminism and Fragility." *Feminist Killjoys*, January 26, 2016. https://feministkilljoys.com/2016/01/26/feminism-and-fragility.

Alba, Avril. *The Holocaust Memorial Museum: Sacred Secular Space*. New York: Palgrave Macmillan, 2015.

American Law Institute. *Model Code of Evidence: As Adopted and Promulgated by the American Law Institute*. Philadelphia: American Law Institute, 1942.

Auslander, Leora. "Beyond Words." *American Historical Review* 110 (October 2005): 1015–45.

Bagnoli, Martina, Holger A. Klein, C. Griffith Mann, and James Robinson, eds. *Treasures of Heaven: Saints, Relics, and Devotion in Medieval Europe*. New Haven: Yale University Press, 2010.

Barthes, Roland. *Camera Lucida*. New York: Hill and Wang, 1981.

Beitman, Ronald S. *Getting Your Hands on the Evidence*. Philadelphia: Ali-Aba Common Continuing, 2005.

Bennett, Jane. *Vibrant Matter: A Political Ecology of Things*. Durham: Duke University Press, 2010.

Berlin, Adele, and Mark Brettler, eds. *The Jewish Study Bible*. Jewish Publication Society Tanakh translation. Oxford: Oxford University Press, 2004.

Biber, Katherine. "The Cultural Afterlife of Criminal Evidence." In *Oxford Research Encyclopedia of Criminology*. April 2017. https://doi.org/10.1093/acrefore/9780190264079.013.160.

Biddick, Kathleen. "Arthur's Two Bodies and the Bare Life of the Archive." In *Cultural Diversity in the British Middle Ages: Archipelago, Island, England*, edited by Jeffrey Jerome Cohen, 117–34. New York: Palgrave Macmillan, 2008.

——. *Make and Let Die: Untimely Sovereignties*. Brooklyn: Punctum Books, 2016.

Blumenthal, David. *Facing the Abusing God: A Theology of Protest*. Louisville: Westminster John Knox Press, 1993.

Bordeleau, Anne, Sascha Hastings, Donald McKay, and Robert Jan van Pelt. *The Evidence Room*. Toronto: New Jewish Press, 2016.

Boscagli, Maurizia. *Stuff Theory: Everyday Objects, Radical Materialism*. London: Bloomsbury, 2014.

Boyle, Katherine. "Auschwitz-Birkenau Barracks at the Holocaust Museum to Be Returned to Poland." *Washington Post*, September 25, 2013.

Boym, Svetlana. *Another Freedom: The Alternative History of an Idea*. Chicago: University of Chicago Press, 2010.

——. *The Future of Nostalgia*. New York: Basic Books, 2001.

Brown, Peter. *The Cult of the Saints: Its Rise and Function in Latin Christianity*. Enl. ed. Chicago: University of Chicago Press, 2015.

Butler, Judith. *Gender Trouble: Feminism and the Subversion of Identity*. New York: Routledge, 1999.

Chiger, Krystyna, with Daniel Paisner. *The Girl in the Green Sweater: A Life in Holocaust's Shadow*. New York: St. Martin's Press, 2008.

Cintron, Enrique. "Some Questions." Paper for Evidence: The Course, spring 2016, Temple University, Religion Department.

Clifton, James. "Conversations in Museums." In *Sensational Religion: Sensory Cultures in Material Practice*, edited by Sally Promey, 205–13. New Haven: Yale University Press, 2014.

Clooney, George, dir. *The Monuments Men*. Culver City, CA: Columbia Pictures / Fox 2000 Pictures, 2014.

Confino, Alon. *Foundational Pasts: The Holocaust as Historical Understanding*. New York: Cambridge University Press, 2011.

Cooke, Rachel. "Maggie Nelson: 'There Is No Catharsis . . . the Stories We Tell Ourselves Don't Heal Us.'" *Guardian*, May 21, 2017.

Crew, Spencer, and James Sims. "Locating Authenticity: Fragments of a Dialogue." In *Exhibiting Cultures: The Poetics and Politics of Museum Display*, edited by Ivan Karp and Steven Lavine, 159–75. Washington, DC: Smithsonian Institution Press, 1991.

Crosby, Christina. *A Body Undone: Living on After Great Pain*. New York: NYU Press, 2016.

Derrida, Jacques. *The Truth in Painting*. Translated by Geoffrey Bennington and Ian McLeod. Chicago: University of Chicago Press, 1987.

Derwin, Susan. "Sense and/or Sensation: The Role of the Body in Holocaust Pedagogy." In *Impossible Images: Contemporary Art After the Holocaust*, edited by Shelley Hornstein, Laura Levitt, and Laurence J. Silberstein, 245–60. New York: NYU Press, 2003.

Diner, Hasia. *We Remember with Love: American Jews and the Myth of Silence After the Holocaust, 1945–1962*. New York: NYU Press, 2009.

Early Jewish Writings. "Jeremiah." http://www.earlyjewishwritings.com/text/jeremiah-jps.html.

Eliade, Mircea. *The Sacred and the Profane: The Nature of Religion*. New York: Harcourt Brace Jovanovich, 1987.

Ellroy, James. *My Dark Place*. New York: Vintage, 1998.

End the Backlog. "What Is the Rape Kit Backlog?" http://www.endthebacklog.org/backlog/what-rape-kit-backlog.

Ezrahi, Sidra. *Booking Passage: Exile and Homecoming in the Modern Jewish Imagination*. Berkeley: University of California Press, 2000.

The Federal Rules of Evidence: 2018 Edition. Grand Rapids: Michigan Legal Publishing, 2017.

Flax, Jane. "The End of Innocence." In *Feminists Theorize the Political*, edited by Judith Butler and Joan Scott, 445–63. New York: Routledge, 1992.

Foer, Jonathan Safran. *Everything Is Illuminated*. New York: Houghton Mifflin, 2002.

Franchot, Jenny. "Unseemly Commemoration: Religion, Fragments, and the Icon." *American Literary History* 9 (Autumn 1997): 502–21.

Freeman, Charles. *Holy Bones, Holy Dust: How Relics Shaped the History of Medieval Europe*. New Haven: Yale University Press, 2011.

Friedländer, Saul. *When Memory Comes*. New York: Farrar, Straus and Giroux, 1979.

Friedman, Michelle. "Reckoning with Ghosts: Second Generation Holocaust Literature and the Labor of Remembrance." PhD diss., Bryn Mawr College, 2001.

Friedman, Richard. *The Elements of Evidence.* 4th ed. Saint Paul: West Academic, 2016.

Gubkin, Liora. *You Shall Tell Your Children: Holocaust Memory in American Passover Ritual.* New Brunswick: Rutgers University Press, 2007.

Guzman, Patricio, dir. *Nostalgia for the Light.* Icarus Films, 2010.

Hahn, Cynthia. *The Reliquary Effect: Enshrining the Sacred Object.* London: Reaktion Books, 2017.

Halsted, Jacob R. *Halsted's Digest of the Law of Evidence.* Ithaca: Cornell University Library, 2009.

Hanley, Julian R., and Wayne W. Schmidt. *Introduction to Criminal Evidence and Court Procedures.* 7th ed. San Pablo, CA: McCutchan, 2011.

Hansen-Glucklich, Jennifer. *Holocaust Memory Reframed: Museums and the Challenges of Representation.* New Brunswick: Rutgers University Press, 2014.

Harris, Gareth. "Edmund de Waal to Create Exhibition in Jewish Ghetto in Venice." *Art Newspaper,* February 12, 2019. https://www.theartnewspaper.com/news/edmund-de-waal-to-create-two-part-exhibition-in-venice-exploring-migration-and-exile.

——. "Writer and Ceramicist Edmund de Waal's Famed Netsuke Collection to Go on Long-Term Loan to Vienna—and Under the Hammer." *Art Newspaper,* October 15, 2018. https://www.theartnewspaper.com/news/writer-and-ceramicist-edmund-de-waal-s-famed-netsuke-collection-go-on-long-term-loan-to-vienna-and-under-the-hammer.

Holland, Agnieszka, dir. *In Darkness.* New York: Sony Pictures Classics, 2011.

Horsman, Yasco. *Theaters of Justice: Judging, Staging, and Working Through in Arendt, Brecht, and Delbo.* Stanford: Stanford University Press, 2010.

Hughes, Jennifer Scheper. "Cradling the Sacred: Image, Ritual, and Affect in Mexican and Mesoamerican Material Religion." *History of Religions* 56 (August 2016): 55–107.

——. "Mysterium Materiae: Vital Matter and the Object as Evidence in the Study of Religion." *Bulletin for the Study of Religion* 41 (November 2012): 16–24.

Iversen, Margaret. *Photography, Trace, and Trauma.* Chicago: University of Chicago Press, 2017.

Jackson, Mick, dir. *Denial.* New York: Bleecker Street Films, 2016.

Jakobsen, Janet. "Queers Are Like Jews, Aren't They? Analogy and Alliance Politics." In *Queer Theory and the Jewish Question,* edited by Daniel Boyarin, Daniel Itzkovitz, and Ann Pellegrini, 64–89. New York: Columbia University Press, 2003.

Kandiyoti, Dalia. "Imagining Cosmopolitanism, Conviviality, and Coexistence in World Literature: Jews, Muslims, Language, and Enchantment in Joann Sfar's *The Rabbi's Cat.*" *Prooftext* 36, nos. 1–2 (2017): 53–82.

Keenan, Thomas, and Eyal Weizman. *Mengele's Skull: The Advent of Forensic Aesthetics.* Berlin: Sternberg Press/Portikus, 2012.

Kennedy, Randy. "Larry Sultan, California Photographer, Dies at 63." *New York Times,* December 14, 2009.

Klepfisz, Irena. "Bashert." In *A Few Words in the Mother Tongue: Poems Selected and New (1971–1990),* 183–200. Portland, OR: Eighth Mountain Press, 1990.

Klinger, Jane E. "Objects of Trauma, Finding the Balance." In *Ethics and Critical Thinking in Conservation,* edited by Pamela Hatchfield, 79–90. Washington, DC: American Institute for Historic and Artistic Conservation, 2013.

Kratsman, Miki. *The Resolution of the Suspect.* Text by Ariella Azoulay. Translated by Tal Haran. Cambridge: Peabody Museum Press, 2016.

Krauss, Nicole. *Great House.* New York: W. W. Norton, 2010.

Kugelmass, Jack, and Jonathan Boyarin, eds. *From a Ruined Garden: The Memorial*

Book of Polish Jewry. Bloomington: Indiana University Press, 1998.

Landy, Joshua, and Michael Saler. "Introduction: The Varieties of Modern Enchantment." In *The Re-enchantment of the World: Secular Magic in a Rational Age*, edited by Joshua Landy and Michael Saler, 1–15. Stanford: Stanford University Press, 2009.

Langer, Lawrence. "The Dilemma of Choice in the Deathcamps." *Centerpoint: A Journal of Interdisciplinary Studies* 4 (Fall 1980): 53–59.

Latta, Joseph. *Property and Evidence by the Book: Everything You Ever Wanted to Know About the Management of a Property and Evidence Room.* Burbank: Evidence Control Systems, 2004.

Latta, Joseph T., and George E. Rush. *Evidence and Property Management.* Incline Village, NV: Copperhouse, 1998.

Levitt, Laura. *American Jewish Loss After the Holocaust.* New York: NYU Press, 2007.

———, ed. "Changing Focus: Family Photography and American Jewish Identity." Special issue, *The Scholar and Feminist Online* 1, no. 3 (2003). http://sfonline.barnard.edu /cf/index.htm.

———. "Evidence: Doing Justice." *Bulletin for the Study of Religion* 41 (November 2012): 37–44.

———. "Holocaust Memory." *Jewish Philosophy Place*, July 1, 2019. https:// jewishphilosophyplace.com/2019/07/01 /holocaust-memory-laura-levitt-guest-blog -the-evidence-room.

———. "Intimate Engagements: A Holocaust Lesson." *Nashim: A Journal of Jewish Women's Studies and Gender Issues* 7 (Spring 2004): 190–205.

———. *Jews and Feminism: The Ambivalent Search for Home.* New York: Routledge, 1997.

———. "Miki Kratsman, Diptych from *The Resolution of the Suspect.*" *MAVCOR Journal* 2, no. 1 (2018). https://doi.org/10 .22332/mav.obj.2018.2.

———. "(The Problem with) Embraces." In *Judaism Since Gender*, edited by Miriam Peskowitz and Laura Levitt, 213–23. New York: Routledge, 1997.

———. "Rescued Evidence: Juridical Justice, Analogy, and the Work of Holocaust Collecting." Paper presented at the Annual Meeting of the Association for Jewish Studies, San Diego, CA, December 2016.

———. "Revenge: 2002." *Nashim: A Journal of Jewish Women's Studies and Gender Issues* 6 (Fall 2003): 35–39.

———. "Revisiting the Property Room: A Humanist Perspective on Doing Justice and Telling Stories." *Conversations: An Online Journal of the Center for the Study of Material and Visual Cultures of Religion* (2015). https://doi.org/10.22332/con.med .2015.1.

———. "The Rites and Rituals of Holding: Revisiting a Holocaust Transgression." "The Transgression Issue," edited by Jonathan M. Hess and Laura S. Lieber. Special issue, *Perspectives* (Spring 2017). http://perspectives.ajsnet.org /transgression-issue/the-rites-and -rituals-of-holding-revisiting-a-holocaust -transgression.

———. "Ritual and Rites in Holocaust Commemoration: A Silence in the Archive." *Bulletin for the Study of Religion*, February 12, 2016. https://bulletin.equinoxpub.com /2016/02/naasr-notes-laura-s-levitt.

———. "Speaking Out of the Silence Around Rape: A Personal Account." *Fireweed: A Feminist Quarterly* 41 (Fall 1993): 20–31.

Limberis, Vasiliki. *Architects of Piety: The Cappadocian Fathers and the Cult of the Martyrs.* New York: Oxford University Press, 2011.

Lindsey, Rachel. *A Communion of Shadows: Religion and Photography in Nineteenth-Century America.* Chapel Hill: University of North Carolina Press, 2017.

Linenthal, Edward T. *Preserving Memory: The Struggle to Create America's Holocaust*

Museum. New York: Columbia University Press, 1995.

Lipstadt, Deborah. *History on Trial: My Day in Court with a Holocaust Denier*. New York: Harper Perennial, 2006.

Liss, Andrea. *Trespassing Through Shadows: Memory, Photography, and the Holocaust*. Minneapolis: University of Minnesota Press, 1998.

Luke, Ben. "'A Moment of Total Crisis in Europe' Prompted Edmund de Waal to Sell His Prized Netsuke Collection." *Art Newspaper*, December 6, 2018. https://www.theartnewspaper.com/news/edmund-de-waal.

Magid, Shaul. "Jewish Renewal and the Holocaust." *Tikkun* 21 (March/April 2006): 59–68.

Mandel, Mike, and Larry Sultan. *Evidence*. Santa Cruz, CA: Clatworthy Colorvues, 1977.

Marks, Laura. *The Skin of Film: Intercultural Cinema, Embodiment, and the Senses*. Durham: Duke University Press, 2000.

McNamara, John. "U.S. Holocaust Museum Research Center Opens in Bowie." *Capital Gazette*, April 24, 2017.

Merritt, Elizabeth E. *National Standards and Best Practices for U.S. Museums*. Washington, DC: AAM Press, 2008.

Morrison, Toni. *Beloved*. New York: Vintage Books, 1987.

Moshenska, Joe. *Iconoclasm as Child's Play*. Stanford: Stanford University Press, 2019.

Nagel, Alexander. "The Afterlife of the Reliquary." In *Treasures of Heaven: Saints, Relics, and Devotion in Medieval Europe*, edited by Martina Bagnoli, Holger A. Klein, C. Griffith Mann, and James Robinson, 211–22. New Haven: Yale University Press, 2010.

Nelson, Maggie. *The Argonauts*. Minneapolis: Graywolf Press, 2015.

——. *Bluets*. Seattle: Wave Books, 2009.

——. *Jane: A Murder*. Berkeley: Soft Skull Press, 2005.

——. *The Red Parts: A Memoir*. New York: Free Press, 2007.

Nichanian, Marc. *The Historiographic Perversion*. Translated by Gil Anidjar. New York: Columbia University Press, 2009.

Nightingale, Andrea. "'Broken Knowledge.'" In *The Re-enchantment of the World: Secular Magic in a Rational Age*, edited by Joshua Landy and Michael Saler, 15–37. Stanford: Stanford University Press, 2009.

——. "On Wandering and Wondering: Theoria in Greek Philosophy and Culture." *Arion: A Journal of Humanities and the Classics* 9 (Fall 2001): 23–58.

Novick, Peter. *The Holocaust in American Life*. Boston: Houghton Mifflin, 1999.

Oksman, Tahneer. "Unframed." Review of *Charlotte Salomon and the Theatre of Memory*, by Griselda Pollock. *Women's Review of Books*, May–June 2018. https://www.wcwonline.org/Women-s-Review-of-Books-May/June-2018/unframed.

Oldenhage, Tania. *Neutestamentliche Passionsgeschichten nach der Shoah: Exegese als Teil der Erinnerungskultur*. Stuttgart: Kohlhammer, 2014.

——. *Parables for Our Time: Rereading New Testament Scholarship After the Holocaust*. New York: Oxford University Press, 2000.

Olin, Margaret. *Touching Photographs*. Chicago: University of Chicago Press, 2012.

Price, Gary. "U.S. Holocaust Memorial Museum Will Build $40 Million Archives and Conservation Center in Suburban DC." *Infodocket*, August 16, 2014. http://www.infodocket.com/2014/08/16/u-s-holocaust-memorial-museum-will-build-40-million-archive-conservation-center-in-suburban-dc.

Promey, Sally, ed. *Sensational Religion: Sensory Cultures in Material Practice*. New Haven: Yale University Press, 2014.

Ratcliff, Carter. "Confronting Evidence." In *Larry Sultan and Mike Mandel*, edited by Galerie Thomas Zander, 201–11. Cologne: Verlag de Buchhandlung Walther König and D.A.P/Distributed Arts, 2012.

Reporting from the Front: Biennale Architecture 2016, 28.05–27.11 Venice. 2 vols. Venice: Marsilio, 2016. Exhibition catalogue.

Rothberg, Michael. Multidirectional Memory: Remembering the Holocaust in the Age of Decolonization. Stanford: Stanford University Press, 2009.

Rubenstein, Mary-Jane. Strange Wonder: The Closure of Metaphysics and the Opening of Awe. New York: Columbia University Press, 2009.

Rush, George E. The Dictionary of Criminal Justice. Guilford, CT: Dushkin, 1994.

Saieh, Nico. "Venice Biennale 2012: Wunderkammer/Tod Williams Billie Tsien Architects." ArchDaily, November 22, 2012. http://www.archdaily.com/272440/venice-biennale-2012-wunderkammer-tod-williams-billie-tsien-architects.

Santner, Eric. Stranded Objects: Mourning, Memory, and Film in Postwar Germany. Ithaca: Cornell University Press, 1990.

Schuessler, Jennifer. "'The Evidence Room': Architects Examine the Horrors of Auschwitz." New York Times, June 15, 2016.

Schwenger, Peter. The Tears of Things: Melancholy and Physical Objects. Minneapolis: University of Minnesota Press, 2006.

Scott, Joan Wallach. "Women's History." In American Feminist Thought at Century's End: A Reader, edited by Linda S. Kauffman, 234–57. Cambridge, MA: Blackwell, 1993.

Shaked, Gershon. The Shadows Within: Essays on Modern Jewish Writers. Philadelphia: Jewish Publication Society, 1987.

Shallcross, Bożena. The Holocaust Object in Polish and Polish-Jewish Culture. Bloomington: Indiana University Press, 2011.

Shandler, Jeffrey. Holocaust Memory in the Digital Age: Survivors' Stories and New Media Practices. Stanford: Stanford University Press, 2017.

Spielberg, Steven, dir. Schindler's List. Universal City, CA: Amblin Entertainment, 1993.

Stallybrass, Peter, and Rosalind Brown. "Fetishizing the Glove in Renaissance Europe." In Things, edited by Bill Brown, 174–92. Chicago: University of Chicago Press, 2004.

Stier, Oren Baruch. Committed to Memory: Cultural Mediations of the Holocaust. Amherst: University of Massachusetts Press, 2003.

——. Holocaust Icons: Symbolizing the Shoah in History and Memory. New Brunswick: Rutgers University Press, 2015.

——. "Torah and Taboo: Containing Jewish Relics and Jewish Identity at the United States Holocaust Memorial Museum." Numen 57, nos. 3–4 (2010): 505–36.

——. "Virtual Memories: Mediating the Holocaust at the Simon Wiesenthal Center's Beit Hashoah–Museum of Tolerance." Journal of the American Academy of Religion 64 (Winter 1996): 831–51.

Ugrešić, Dubravka. The Museum of Unconditional Surrender. Translated by Celia Hawkesworth. New York: New Directions Books, 1996.

Waal, Edmund de. The Hare with Amber Eyes: A Hidden Inheritance. New York: Picador, 2010.

——. The White Road: Journey into an Obsession. New York: Farrar, Straus and Giroux, 2015.

Waal, Elizabeth de. The Exiles Return. New York: Picador, 2014.

Waldman, Ayelet. Love and Treasure. New York: Knopf, 2014.

Ward, Philip. The Nature of Conservation: A Race Against Time. Los Angeles: Getty Conservation Institute, 2010. https://www.getty.edu/conservation/publications_resources/pdf_publications/pdf/nature_cons_en_full.pdf.

Weissberg, Liliane. "Memory Confined." In *Cultural Memory and the Construction of Identity*, edited by Dan Ben-Amos and Liliane Weissberg, 45–76. Detroit: Wayne State University Press, 1999.

Wiesel, Elie. *Night*. New York: Bantam Books, 1982.

Wigmore, John Henry. *A Treatise on the System of Evidence in Trials at Common Law*. Vol. 1, *Including the Statutes and Judicial Decisions of All Jurisdictions of the States, England, and Canada*. London: Forgotten Books, 2017.

Williams, Tod, and Billie Tsien. *Wunderkammer*. New Haven: Yale University Press, 2012.

Winnicott, D. W. "Fear of Breakdown." *International Review of Psychoanalysis* 1 (1974): 103–7.

——. "The Psychology of Madness: A Contribution from Psycho-Analysis." In *Psycho-Analytic Explorations*, edited by Clare Winnicott, Ray Shepherd, and Madeleine Davis, 119–29. New York: Routledge, 2018.

Winslow, Emily. "The Saga of My Rape Kit." *New York Times*, June 5, 2016.

Wisniewski, Robert. *The Beginnings of the Cult of Relics*. New York: Oxford University Press, 2019.

Woolf, Virginia. *A Room of One's Own*. New York: Harcourt, Brace & World, 1929.

——. *To the Lighthouse*. New York: Harcourt, Brace & World, 1927. Reprint, Ware, Hertfordshire: Wordsworth Classics, 1994.

Wypijewski, JoAnn, ed. *Painting by Numbers: Komar and Melamid's Scientific Guide to Art*. New York: Farrar, Straus and Giroux, 1997.

Yerebakan, Osman Can. "The Artist Making Installations Out of Rape Kits." *Cut*, January 15, 2019. https://www.thecut.com/2019/01/aliza-shvarts-rape-kit-exhibition-is-a-sad-american-picture.html.

Yerushalmi, Yosef Hayim. *Zakhor: Jewish History and Jewish Memory*. Seattle: University of Washington Press, 1996.

Young, James. *The Texture of Memory: Holocaust Memorials and Meaning*. New Haven: Yale University Press, 1994.

——. *Writing and Rewriting the Holocaust: Narrative and the Consequences of Interpretation*. Bloomington: Indiana University Press, 1988.

Young, Stephenie. "Geographies of Loss: Testimony, Art, and the Afterlife of Batajnica's Disappeared Objects." *Getuigen tussen Geschiedenis en Herinnering* 126 (April 2018): 152–57.

Yuval, Israel Jacob. *Two Nations in Your Womb: Perceptions of Jews and Christians in Late Antiquity and the Middle Ages*. Berkeley: University of California Press, 2006.

Index